Macmillan English

Language Book

3

Mary Bowen

Louis Fidge

Liz Hocking

Wendy Wren

MACMILLAN

Scope and sequence: Units 1-9

FLUENCY BOOK 3		LANGUAGE BOOK 3		
		Reading and understanding	**Working with words**	**Sentence building**
		REVISION		
Unit 1	*This is Tex*	reading text: *Professor Inkspot's telescope* text type: story with clear beginning, middle and end	mechanisms	punctuating direct speech
Unit 2	*Up in space*	reading text: *Chinese dragons* text type: descriptive information	descriptive sentences	using conjunctions *and* and *but*
Unit 3	*The first key*	reading text: *The Aztecs of Central America* text type: factual information	past tenses	pluralising nouns ending with vowel + y and consonant + y
		REVISION: UNITS 1-3		
Unit 4	*In the desert*	reading text: *Animals in the Gobi desert* text type: information and labelled pictures	desert animals	pluralising nouns ending with *f* or *fe*
Unit 5	*Yorgi's house*	reading text: *The horse race* text type: story with a strong opening	verbs for animal movements	punctuating sentences – full stops, question and exclamation marks
Unit 6	*A very long time ago*	reading text: *Ice age giants* text type: information	animal parts	past tense of some irregular verbs
		REVISION: UNITS 4-6		
Unit 7	*The big balloon*	reading text: *Birds in the air; Did you see it?* text type: poems	matching animals with verbs; definitions	collective nouns
Unit 8	*Pirates!*	reading text: *Holiday island* text type: dialogue	adjectives	adding *ing* to cvc verbs (hop – hopping) and magic **e** verbs (take – taking)
Unit 9	*Jack*	reading text: *A letter from a sailor* text type: a letter	adjectives	adding *ed* to cvc verbs (rip – ripped) and magic **e** verbs (smile – smiled)
		REVISION: UNITS 7-9		

Grammar	Listening	Spelling	Class writing
REVISION			
There were buttons on the machine. There was a handle, too. Professor Inkspot pushed the buttons. Then he pulled the handle.	What did he see? (identifying descriptions)	**oo** (short sound as in **cook**)	simple story with clear beginning, middle and end
A dragon and a king met every night. The dragon had nine heads. The king told the dragon about his problems.	The poor man and the dragon. (listening for detail)	**u** (short sound as in **bull**)	description of a dragon
Did the Aztecs live in Central America? Their books did not have words in them.	Who is speaking? (identifying characters)	**ea** (short sound as in **head**; long sound as in **peach**)	information about Aztec children
REVISION: UNITS 1-3			
A camel is as strong as a yak. A gazelle is faster than a snow leopard.	Two brothers. (identifying characters; listening for detail)	**y** sounding **ee** as in **jelly**	labelling and describing an animal
Shirav was the fastest rider in the valley. Sukhe's horse was the strongest.	Who is speaking? (identifying family members)	**oi** and **oy**	choosing a strong opening and finishing a story
The mammoth was the most enormous animal on land. The sabre-tooth cat was more dangerous than a tiger. A is good. B is better. C is the best. D is bad. E is worse. F is the worst.	Extraordinary animals. (listening for descriptive detail)	**aw** (sounding **or** as in **claw**)	information about an animal
REVISION: UNITS 4-6			
The birds are going to fly over the snow. The balloon is going to rise into the sky.	A holiday on Coconut Island. (identifying locations on a map)	**air** and **are** (sounding **air** as in **glare**)	completing a rhyming poem
You must be careful! You mustn't climb on the rocks.	What must they take? (listening for detail)	**ew** (sounding **oo** as in **grew**)	completing a dialogue
Tom wanted to touch the spines. Why were they dangerous? They were dangerous because they had poison in them.	Hats and monkeys. (listening to and retelling a story)	**wh** words	a letter
REVISION: UNITS 7-9			

Scope and sequence: Units 10-18

FLUENCY BOOK 3		LANGUAGE BOOK 3		
		Reading and understanding	Working with words	Sentence building
Unit 10	*What a trip*	reading text: *Pictures* text type: information	opposite meanings of adjectives	adverbs of manner ending *ly* e.g. slowly
Unit 11	*Under the sea*	reading text: *The diving lesson* text type: story with a strong setting	verbs for sound and movement	the importance of verbs in sentences
Unit 12	*The wreck*	reading text: *Coral reefs* text type: information	types of fish and coral	comparative adjectives ending consonant + y, e.g. tiny – tinier
REVISION: UNITS 10-12				
Unit 13	*The flower seller*	reading text: *My diary* text type: descriptions of people	personal description	personal pronouns
Unit 14	*The chariot race*	reading text: *The Romans* text type: information, diagrams and labelled pictures	opposite meanings	past tense verbs ending vowel + y, (play – played) and consonant + y (carry – carried)
Unit 15	*Be careful, Mobi!*	reading text: *Delicious ice cream* text type: poems	*a* or *an* preceding adjectives (e.g. an open door, a red door)	*a / an* + adjective + noun
REVISION: UNITS 13-15				
Unit 16	*Mobi and the crystals*	reading text: *Glass* text type: information and instructions for making things	glass objects	using conjunctions *because* and *so*
Unit 17	*A clever elephant*	reading text: *Eddie, the Emerald Island Detective* text type: strip story	words with similar meanings	superlative adjectives, e.g. tall – tallest
Unit 18	*Gloomdrop's box*	reading text: *The selfish giant* text type: descriptive story	verbs and adverbs	direct speech – with reporting clause at beginning or end
REVISION: UNITS 16-18				

Grammar	Listening	Spelling	Class writing
The girl was playing the piano. The children were painting.	Put the pictures in the correct order. (sequencing)	**ph** words	description of actions in a photograph
While Uncle Roy was tidying up the hut, Andy was swimming.	Complete the song. (listening for detail)	compound words	a story with two different settings
Fishermen can damage the coral. The coral died. Nobody could find out why.	What could they do? (listening for detail; identifying activities)	suffix **ful**	description of a coral reef
REVISION: UNITS 10-12			
Is there any water? There isn't any water. There is some water. Has she got any gloves? She hasn't got any gloves. She has got some gloves.	How many mistakes did she make? (listening for detail)	prefix **un**	describing a person's appearance
How many people watched the races? Lots of/A lot of people. How much time did they spend there? Lots of/A lot of time.	Name the charioteers. Who won the race?(logic puzzle; following a sequence of actions)	prefix **dis**	labelling pictures and describing them
Would you like a lolly? The lolly in your hand is melting. I love ice cream. The ice cream in this café is delicious.	Make an ice cream surprise! (following a recipe; sequencing)	**c** sounding **s** as in **mice**	completing a rhyming poem
REVISION: UNITS 13-15			
Roman glass was often/usually/always beautiful. Painters sometimes paint glass. You must never drop a glass bottle.	What is Professor Inkspot talking about?(listening for detail)	suffix **er** as in **painter**	instructions for making a necklace
Can we help you? Can I look in your suitcase?	Who stole Mrs Moneypot's necklace? (following directions)	syllables	speech bubbles for a strip story
The wind blew fiercely/more fiercely/the most fiercely.	Who are friends? (listening for detail)	**ch** words	a descriptive story
REVISION: UNITS 16-18			

Revision

1 Listen and find the people. 🎧

| Jim | Mr Carter | Mrs Carter | Joe | Lily |
| Miss Hill | Max | Tom | Andy | Mrs White |

Today

2 Whose are these things?

Revision *present tense; possessions*

3 What are they doing?
What are they wearing?

4 Who likes these things?

1 Find the people. Who was in the market yesterday? Who worked yesterday?

Yesterday

2 Listen. Who said this?

Revision *past tense of* to be; *regular past tense verbs*

3 What was it like in the city yesterday?

4 Was there a lot of traffic? What was there?

Professor Inkspot's telescope

Bang!

Billy woke up with a start. He looked at the clock. It was half past six. BANG! Billy jumped out of bed and ran to the window. Next door he could see Professor Inkspot's shed. There was a small cloud of blue smoke above the shed. Billy saw a green flashing light. Fizzzz! Pop! Bang! The light changed to red. Billy got dressed quickly and ran round to Professor Inkspot's shed.

'Are you there, Professor?' he shouted. A strange whirring sound began. A bell rang and an orange light turned to green.

'It works!' a voice exclaimed.

'Professor,' Billy called, 'is that you?'

'Of course it's me!' said the voice. 'Come in, Billy, come in!' Billy stepped slowly forwards and went inside.

Professor Inkspot stood next to a strange machine. On the front were four large dials with numbers. Below the dials were several bright red buttons. In the middle was a square screen. Beside the screen was a handle. Under the screen was a row of switches.

'What is it?' Billy asked.

'It's an inter-active space telescope,' replied the professor. 'It shows you what is happening in space! Do you want to see it work?'

'Yes, please,' said Billy.

'Look here,' said the professor, 'you turn this … and press these … and pull those upwards … .' For several minutes the professor was busy. His hands moved quickly over the machine. Billy waited quietly and watched. At last the professor turned round. 'It's ready!' he said.

 Parents: *see extra material on page 166*

Professor Inkspot pulled the handle downwards. A red light came on. He turned a dial. It clicked noisily. Then there was a loud buzzing sound. Billy jumped backwards.

'Don't worry!' shouted the professor. 'Look at the screen.'

Billy saw small people in spacesuits. There were trees but they were blue and yellow. The sky was bright pink. It was another planet!

The professor pointed to a tree. 'Watch this!' he said. He pushed a button. Suddenly the tree filled the screen. Billy saw a very strange silver bird in it.

'Let's look at the people,' said the professor. 'Press that switch.' Billy pressed. At once the people on the screen were big.

Billy gasped. 'I know those people,' he said.

'What?' said the professor, in surprise.

'Yes,' said Billy, 'Those are the people in my favourite TV programme, *Adventures in space*. This isn't an inter-active telescope, professor. It's an inter-active TV!'

Reading and understanding

1 **Complete the sentences.**

1 Billy woke up at half past _six_ .
2 He woke up because he heard a loud _Bang_.
3 Billy went inside Professor Inkspot's _shed_ .
4 Professor Inkspots machine shows what is happening in _____ .
5 When Professor Inkspot pulled the _____ , a red light came on.
6 Billy saw a _____ bird in the tree.
7 The people on the _____ were from a TV programme.

2 **Circle the best word to complete each sentence.**

1 Professor Inkspot works in a   shop   (shed)   ship.
2 Billy saw a cloud of   smells   smiles   (smoke.)
3 He   **heard**   (saw)   smelled   flashing lights.
4 He   (heard)   saw   found   a strange whirring sound.
5 There was a square   scream   green   (screen)   in the middle of the machine.

3 **Which way is Billy jumping? Write the directions.**

| forwards   downwards   upwards   backwards |

1 _downwards_ 2 _forwards_ 3 _backwards_ 4 _upwards_

Get active 1

Comprehension focus   *Consolidation of new language in* Professor Inkspot's telescope

Working with words

1 **Write the adverbs.**

> quickly   slowly   noisily   quietly

1 _noisly_ : making a lot of sound   2 _quickly_ : at a fast speed
3 _quitely_ : making very little noise   4 _slowly_ : not quickly

2 **Write the verb. Write the noun.**

> turn   pull   push   press

      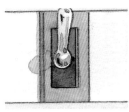   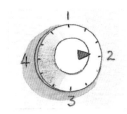

1 _pull_   2 _press_   3 _push_   4 _turn_
  lever   _button_   _handle_   _timer_

Sentence building

This is my space telescope.

*Remember! When we write what a person says, we put it in **speech marks**.*

This is a **sentence**.

'This is my space telescope,' the Professor said.

We must put a **comma** here.   We end it with a **full stop**.

1 **Discuss what punctuation marks are missing. Put them in.**

1 My name is Professor Inkspot, the man said.
2 I went to see the Professor, Billy said.
3 I am in the shed, Professor Inkspot said.
4 Your machine looks good, Billy said.
5 Don't touch it, the professor said

Grammar

Do you remember Professor Inkspot's strange machine?

Below the dials were several buttons.

Beside the screen was a handle.

Professor Inkspot pushed the buttons.

Then he pulled the handle.

1 Read and circle true (T) or false (F).

1 Billy jumped out of bed at half past seven.   T   (F)
2 There was a machine in Professor Inkspot's garden.   (T)   F
3 Billy stepped inside the shed.   (T)   F
4 There were bright green buttons on the machine.   T   (F)
5 Billy watched the professor.   (T)   F

2 Correct the false sentences. Say. Then write.

3 Fill the gaps with verbs from the box. Use the past tense.

ask   gasp   ~~turn~~   ~~wait~~
look   ~~move~~   press   point

Billy __waited__ quietly. The professor's hands __turn__ over the buttons and dials. At last he __more__ round and __point__ to the machine. 'Can you see that switch?' he __ask__. 'Press it, please.' Billy __press__ the switch. He __look__ at the screen.

'Oh!' he __gasp__ in surprise. 'I know those people!'

Grammar focus   *past simple affirmative of* to be *and regular verbs*

Listening

What a fantastic machine!

1 What did Professor Inkspot see on his screen? Listen and write the numbers.

 A

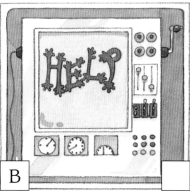 B

 C

 D

 E

2 Listen and chant.

Blast Off!

Smoke billows
Flames spurt
Engines roar
Ears hurt
10 9 8 7 6 5 4 3 2 1 ZERO. LIFT OFF!
Ground shakes
Crowd cheers
Rocket climbs
And disappears.

Veronica Clark

Listening focus *identifying descriptions*

Spelling

 In some words the **oo** makes a short sound.

He **loo**ked at the clock.

1 Listen and read.

The cook took a look at the book.

Write the words in the sentence which make the same sound as **cook**.

Took _____ look _____ book _____

2 Say the sounds. Make the words.

   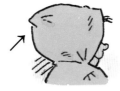   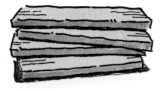

f → oo → t   h → oo → d   w → oo → d

foot _____   hood _____   wood _____

3 Write.

1    2

I like this book .   My foot hurts!

4 Tick ✓ the words you can read.

cook ✓ look ✓ book ✓ foot ✓ hood ✓ wood ✓

Class writing

Let's write a story.

1 Look at the pictures. Answer the questions. Write the story.

Beginning

1

What did Billy see?
What was it like?

2

What did Billy do?

Middle

3

What happened?
Who was in the box?

4

What did Professor
Inkspot do?

5

What did Billy
do then?

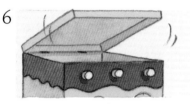

6

What happened?
Was Professor
Inkspot inside?

7

Where did Billy look?
Was Professor
Inkspot there?

8

What did Billy do?

End

9

What did Billy
do next?

10

What happened?

11

Who or what was
in the box?

Chinese Dragons 🎧

Chinese people love dragons. They have many stories about them. In the stories the dragons came from the rivers. They brought water for plants, animals and people. That is why Chinese people like them. In China, you can see them everywhere; on buildings, on bridges, on gates, on chairs, on vases and on clothes.

The king of the dragons was very strong. It looked like lots of different animals. It had a head like a camel and horns like a goat. It had the small ears of a bull. Its neck and body were like a lizard's body. It had green fish scales from its head to its tail. It had the paws of a tiger and the sharp claws of an eagle.

Dragons were usually greenish. Another kind of dragon was green on its back, yellow at the sides and red underneath. Sometimes a dragon was blue all over. A dragon could be huge like an elephant or it could be small like a tiny lizard.

 Parents: *see extra material on page 166*

In Chinese pictures some dragons have wings. Sometimes a dragon is thin like a snake. Sometimes they are fat and they look like giant frogs with tails. They can have long beards and bushy eyebrows. They can look very fierce. Dragons can breathe fire but they do not hurt people. Usually they help them and Chinese people think that their dragons are beautiful, friendly and wise.

In one old Chinese story a dragon with nine heads helped the king. Every night the dragon and the king met at the top of a golden tower. The king told the dragon about the problems in his country. The dragon helped the king to think wisely. The people were happy because they had a good king.

Chinese emperors had dragons on their beds, on their thrones and on their boats. When someone called the emperor 'dragon-face' he was very happy. The Chinese princesses had dragons on their dresses. They told each other stories about helpful, friendly dragons.

This dress belonged to a Chinese empress. The dragon has a big head with horns and whiskers. It has fish scales and spines on its thin body. It has five short legs and claws on each foot. Flames are coming from its body. There is yellow on this dress because it was for a empress. Only the emperor's family had yellow on their clothes.

Reading and understanding

1 Circle the best word to complete each sentence.

1 In Chinese stories dragons brought (rivers) water.

2 Dragons can breathe water (fire).

3 Sometimes dragons have long (beards) eyelashes.

4 Dragons usually (help) hurt people.

5 Chinese emperors had dragons on their (thrones) faces.

6 The emperor's family could wear yellow (beautiful) clothes.

2 Read the questions. Tick ✓ your answers.

1 Which animals was the king dragon like?

cat ☐ camel ✓ lion ☐ sheep ☐

bull ✓ crocodile ☐ lizard ✓

2 Which words described Chinese dragons?

fierce ☐ careful ☐ friendly ✓

helpful ☐ wet ☐ wise ✓

3 Which things did some dragons have?

wings ☐ spots ☐ fingers ☐ feet ☐

horns ✓ claws ☐

4 Which of these animals were in the information about dragons?

Get active 2

Working with words

1 **Find and write the correct word.**

fierce wise throne huge hurt

1 An emperor has a special chair. It is a ___throne___ .

2 When a lion or a tiger shows its teeth, it looks ___fierce___ .

3 An older person often knows a lot and is very ___wise___ !

4 Some spiders look scary but usually they do not ___hurt___ people.

5 Some dragons are tiny but some of them are ___huge___ .

Sentence building

> Remember! A **conjunction** can **join** **two sentences together**.

This dragon is green. It has a long tail.
This dragon is green **and** it has a long tail.

This dragon breathes fire. It does not hurt people.
This dragon breathes fire **but** it does not hurt people.

1 **Underline the conjunctions. Discuss which two sentences each conjunction joins.**

1 The dragon had paws <u>and</u> it had sharp claws.

2 Some dragons are green <u>but</u> some are blue.

3 I sat on the chair <u>and</u> I read a book.

4 The door is open <u>but</u> the window is shut.

5 I got my spellings right <u>but</u> Tom got all his spellings wrong.

6 The wind blew <u>and</u> it rained hard.

Grammar

A dragon and a king met every night.

The dragon had nine heads.

The king told the dragon about his problems.

1 Find the past tenses. All the words are in the word snake.
Say. Then write.

rancameflewsawtoldheardmetwenthad

1 tell _told_   2 meet _met_   3 come _came_

4 go _went_   5 have _had_   6 run _ran_

7 see _saw_   8 fly _flew_   9 hear _heard_

2 Was Mobi right? Correct his mistakes.
Say. Then write.

10.12.10

*I met a dragon with ~~three heads~~. It was red and black.
It had two long tails. It ran along the ground on six short
legs. Then it flew through the air with four big wings.
It opened its mouth and blue flames came out.*

Listening

Here's a story about a dragon.

1 Look at the pictures. Talk about them.

2 Look at the pictures and listen to the story.

3 Answer these questions.

1 Was the family rich or poor?
2 Did the dragon live in a house or in a cave?
3 The dragon had a thorn. Was it in its wing or in its foot?
4 Who helped the dragon? Was he frightened? Was he brave?
  Was he kind?
5 What was inside the box?
6 Who brought the box to the family?
7 Was the dragon fierce or kind?

4 Can you tell the story?

5 Listen and chant.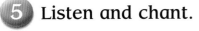

Red dragon... Green dragon... Gold dragon... Blue dragon... ROAR!

16-12-10

Spelling

Listen to the sound the **u** makes in **bull**.

The king of dragons had the small ears of a **bull**.

1 Say the sounds. Write the words.

1 p → u → ll

Pull

2 b → u → ll

bull

3 p → u → sh

push

4 b → u → sh

bush

5 p → u → t

put

2 Say the sounds. Make the words. Write.

1

p → u → ll _pull_

2

p → u → sh _push_

3

b → u → sh _bush_

4

b → u → ll _bull_

3 Tick ✓ the words you can read.

pull ☑ bull ☑ push ☑ bush ☑ put ☑

17-12-10

Spelling focus *words with a short* **u** *sound*

Class writing

Let's write about this dragon!

A long time ago, this Chinese dragon lived in a big river.

What colour was it? Was it big? What could it do?

Did it look like any of these animals?

Did it have any of these? claws? horns? teeth? wings?
What were they like?

What did it look like? Was it scary? fierce? friendly? funny?

Choose some words. Write them down.

Write about the dragon.

The Aztecs of Central America

1 Where did the Aztecs come from?

The first people in America came from Asia. They arrived about 30,000 years ago. They did not have houses. They lived in tents. When there was no grass for their animals, they moved on.

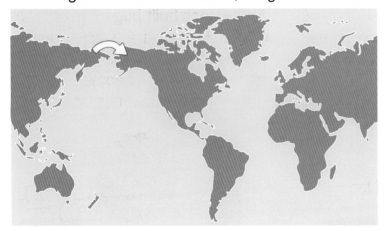

Thousands of years passed. People learned to grow plants. They built houses and they made farms. About eight hundred years ago, the Aztec people came to the middle of America.

3 What did the Aztecs do?

They built gardens in the lake. They made four walls with sticks and put mud inside. Then they grew plants in the mud. They travelled between the gardens in boats.

They looked under the ground for special stones. These stones were different colours – green, turquoise, orange and red. They cut the stones out of the rock and made jewels.

5 What did Aztec children do?

Little children helped in the house. Boys carried water and girls swept the floor. Later, boys learned their fathers' work. This boy is the son of a basket maker. He is learning to make baskets.

Children of important families went to school. Sometimes clever children from ordinary families went to school, too. They learned about the stars and they learned to count and write. All children worked hard.

Parents: see extra material on page 166

2 Where did the Aztecs live?

They built houses on an island in a lake. They built bridges across the lake to the island. One bridge carried fresh water to the island. This kind of bridge is an aqueduct.

The Aztecs built huge pyramids on the island. There were palaces around the pyramids and houses for important people. The poor people had small houses with mud walls and grass roofs.

4 What did the Aztecs like?

They liked gold jewellery with coloured jewels and stones. They liked coloured feathers. They wore beautiful feathers on their heads. This headdress belonged to a king.

On special days the important people carried long sticks with feathers. They wore beautiful clothes. Sometimes their clothes had feathers on, too. The ladies wore long skirts and sandals on their feet.

6 What was Aztec writing like?

The Aztecs had books but the books did not have words in them. They had many small pictures. The pictures told a story or gave information. In school, children learned to understand these pictures.

7 What happened to the Aztecs?

For two hundred years, the Aztecs were strong and powerful. Then, five hundred years ago people from Europe sailed to America. They fought the Aztecs and won. They captured the city and the king.

Reading and understanding

1 **Read and circle true (T) or false (F).**

1 The Aztecs came from Australia.   T   F
2 They made their home on an island.   T   F
3 They built houses on a hill.   T   F
4 They had gardens next to the lake.   T   F
5 Aztec ladies wore sandals on their feet.   T   F
6 All the Aztec children went to school.   T   F
7 They had books without pictures.   T   F

2 **Complete the sentences.**

1 The first people in America lived in __tent__.

2 The Aztec people made their home in the __mud__ of America.

3 They build __briduge__ across the lake to the island.

4 In school children learned about the __stars__.

5 Aztec books had many different __picture__ in them.

3 **Write the words.**

1 hat mad of fathers

2 ctpensekshouse

3 pirduge

4 baskets

5 faethers

Get active 3

Working with words

1 Choose the correct past tense from the box. Write it next to the present tense verb.

carried wore built made swept fought cut

1 build _built_   2 fight _fought_   3 cut _cut_

4 wear _wore_   5 sweep _swept_   6 carry _carried_

7 make _made_

Sentence building

Remember! **Singular** *means* **one**. **Plural** *means* **more than one**.

Rule 1
If a noun ends with a **vowel + y**, we add **s** to make it plural.

a boy   two boys

Rule 2
If a noun ends with a **consonant + y**, we change the **y** to **i**, and add **es**.

a lady   two ladies

1 What is the plural of each word? Discuss which rule you use.

1
one baby   two _babies_

2
one key   two _keys_

3
one toy   two _toys_

4
one fly   two _flies_

5
one lorry   two _lorries_

6
one trolley   two _trolleys_

17.01.11

Grammar

What do you remember about the Aztecs?

Did they live in Central America?

Did they build pyramids?

They built big houses but poor people did not live in them.

They had books but the books did not have words in them.

1 **Ask questions about the Aztecs.** *Did they ... ?*
Answer *Yes, they did.* **or** *No, they didn't.*

1 ... live in Africa?　　2 ... live in America?　　3 ... like gold and jewels?

4 ... build pyramids?　　5 ... wear jeans and T-shirts?　　6 ... wear clothes with feathers?

2 **Read and circle true (T) or false (F).**

1	The Aztecs lived in Europe.	T	F
2	They built gardens and grew plants.	T	F
3	They found jewels in lakes.	T	F
4	Girls learned their fathers' work.	T	F
5	All children went to school.	T	F
6	The Aztecs had books.	T	F
7	Their books had words.	T	F
8	People from Africa fought the Aztecs.	T	F

3 **Correct the false sentences.**
Use *did not* **and the verbs in the box.**

learn	live	have	fight	find	go

Grammar focus　*past simple interrogative and negative*

Listening

3

Listen to the Aztecs!

1 **Look at these pictures of people from the time of the Aztecs. Talk about the pictures.**

A    B    C

D    E    F

2 **Listen. Who is speaking?**

1 _____   2 _____

3 _____   4 _____

5 _____   6 _____

3 **Listen and sing.**

Canoe Song

My paddle's keen and bright,
Flashing with silver,
Follow the wild goose flight,
Dip, dip and swing

Dip, dip and swing her back,
Flashing with silver,
Follow the wild goose flight,
Dip, dip and swing.

Margaret Embers McGee

Listening focus   *identifying characters*

31

Spelling

The letters **ea** in some words can make a long sound like **ee**.

leaves    jeans

The letters **ea** in some words can also make a sound like a **short e**.
The Aztecs liked coloured **feathers**.

1 **Say the sounds. Write the words.**

1

br → ea → d

bread

2

h → ea → d

head

3

sw → ea → ter

sweater

4

thr → ea → d

thread

2 **Use the correct word from the box to complete each sentence.**

| ready   healthy   weather   feathers |

1 In the morning I get ___*ready*___ to go to school.
2 The ___*weather*___ is very hot today.
3 Aztecs liked coloured ___*feathers*___ .
4 Fruit and vegetables keep you ___*healthy*___ .

3 **Tick ✓ the words you can read.**

bread ☐   sweater ☐   weather ☐   feathers ☐
ready ☐   healthy ☐   head ☐   thread ☐

Class writing

Let's write about Aztec children!

Aztec children worked hard. What did they do? Where did they work?
Write about them.

grow   cut   go

the boys grow
a flowr and cut
them then they goin their hous

help   sweep

girls help
her mum and
weep the house

study   count

the children
of important familes
are studying counting and
learning a lots of things.

write   look   understand

the children
are writing an
look at the work
and then they
under stand.

Revision 1
You can do it!

1 **Look at the map.**
Have you got friends or family in any of these places?
What do you know about these places?

2 **Listen and read.** 🎧

3 **Read and say.**
1 Which city had tall buses?
2 Where did Billy see camels?
3 Which place was cold?
4 Where did they go in a plane?
5 Where did they see animals jumping?
6 What did they run along?
7 Which city had a tall tower?
8 Which country had a lost city?

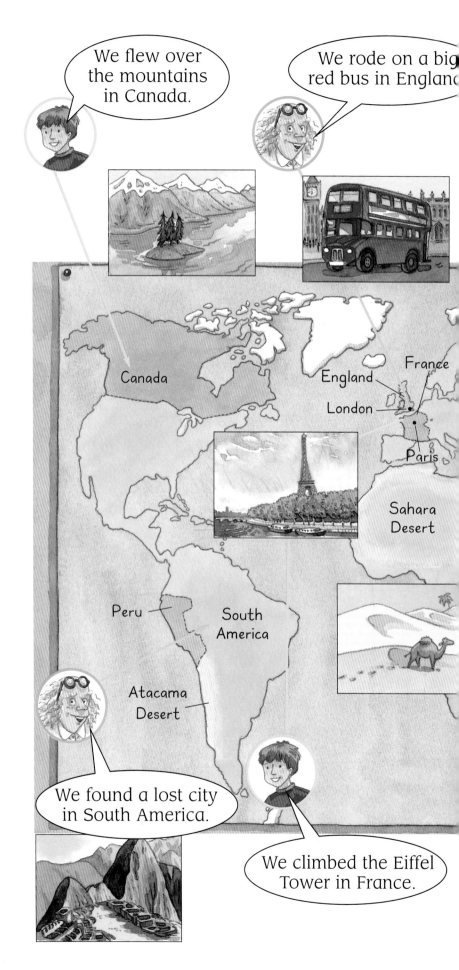

We flew over the mountains in Canada.

We rode on a big red bus in England

We found a lost city in South America.

We climbed the Eiffel Tower in France.

Canada

England
France
London
Paris

Sahara Desert

Peru
South America

Atacama Desert

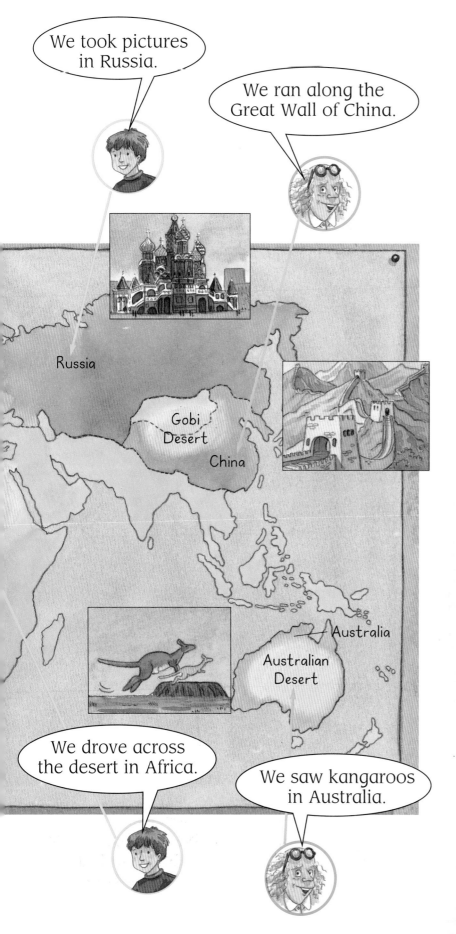

We took pictures in Russia.

We ran along the Great Wall of China.

Russia

Gobi Desert

China

Australia

Australian Desert

We drove across the desert in Africa.

We saw kangaroos in Australia.

4 **Answer the questions.**
1 Did they drive along the Great Wall?
2 Did they fly over the desert?
3 Did they see camels in Australia?
4 How many deserts are on the map?

5 **Listen and say which place.** 🎧

6 **Act out the story.**

7 **Write the words.**

_____   _____

_____   _____

_____   _____

Animals in the Gobi Desert

Herd animals

The herdsmen in the Gobi desert look after thousands of sheep, goats, camels and yaks. In the spring they take their herds of animals up the hills to the new grass. In the autumn they go down to the valley again. These herdsmen take their tents with them. They load pieces of the tent onto the camels. They carry the heavy loads on their backs. Camels are as strong as yaks.

Bactrian camel

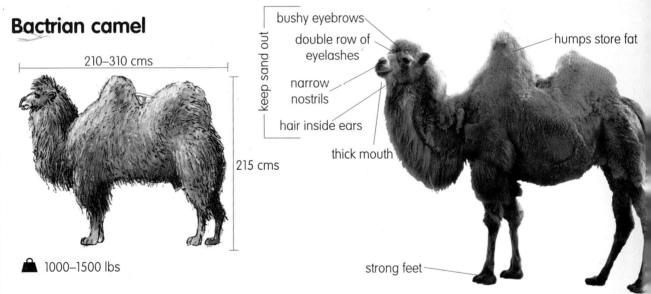

210–310 cms

215 cms

1000–1500 lbs

keep sand out

bushy eyebrows

double row of eyelashes

humps store fat

narrow nostrils

hair inside ears

thick mouth

strong feet

This camel can live in the desert for many weeks without food or water. It lives off the fat in its humps and water in its body. When a camel fills up with water, it drinks 150 litres (30 gallons). It can drink all this in 10 minutes. It can eat plants with sharp thorns and spikey leaves. Bactrian camels have long thick hair in winter. In the summer their winter coats drop off. There are not many wild camels in the Gobi desert. Most of them are looked after by herdsmen.

Wild animals

These are gazelles. They are wild animals. This means that they find their own food.
People do not take them to new grass. They are very fast animals. A new baby gazelle
cannot walk at all. After one or two days it can jump. When it is 10 days old it can leap at
40 kph. That is faster than a man can run. An adult gazelle leaps across the desert at
more than 60 kph. It is faster than a snow leopard.

The snow leopard

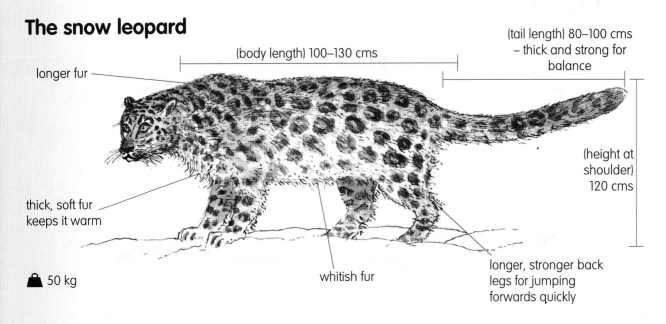

(body length) 100–130 cms

(tail length) 80–100 cms
– thick and strong for
balance

longer fur

(height at
shoulder)
120 cms

thick, soft fur
keeps it warm

50 kg

whitish fur

longer, stronger back
legs for jumping
forwards quickly

There are 4,000 – 7,000 snow leopards in the world. About 1,000 live in the mountains of
the Gobi desert. They hunt alone for wild sheep and goats. They hide among the rocks and
small bushes. Snow leopards never attack people. In winter the snow lies deep and the
snow leopard's light grey fur helps it to hide. In the past, men hunted snow leopards for
their beautiful fur but now these animals are protected.

Reading and understanding

1 **Choose the correct ending.**

1 The herdsmen have lots of sheep and __goats__. a gazelles b goats
2 The herdsmen go down to the valley in the __spring__. a autumn
  b spring
3 A thirsty camel can drink __100__. a 100 litres b 150 litres
4 An adult gazelle can leap at __65__. a 60 kph b 65 kph
5 Snow leopards live in the __valleys__. a valleys b mountains
6 The snow leopard's grey fur helps it to __jump__. a hide b jump

2 **Complete the sentences.**

1 The herdsmen take their __tents__ with them.

2 Camels are as strong as __yaks__.

3 A Bactrian camel has __two__ humps.

4 Gazelles are __weaked__ animals.

5 An adult gazelle is __faster__ than a snow leopard.

3 **Discuss this question.**

Is it sometimes cold in the Gobi desert? How do you know?

4 **Tick ✓ the animals that live in the Gobi desert.**

Get active 4

Comprehension focus Consolidation of new language in Animals in the Gobi Desert

Working with words

1 **Read the clues. Write the words.**

1 It is faster than a snow leopard.
2 It is as big as a zebra.
   You can ride on it.
3 It has very long horns.
4 Herdsmen look after it.
   It is usually brown.
5 It has two humps.
6 It hunts alone.
7 Herdsmen look after it. It is usually white.

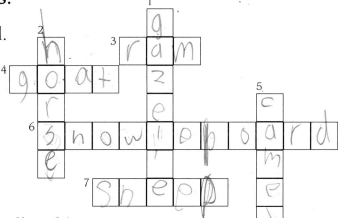

Crossword answers filled in:
1 down: g a z e l l e
2 down: h o r s e
3 across: r a m
4 across: g o a t
5 down: c a m e l
6 across: s n o w l e o p a r d
7 across: s h e e p

Sentence building

Remember! **Singular** means **one**. **Plural** means **more than one**.

Rule

If a noun ends with **f** (or **fe**) we change the f (or fe) to **v** and add **es** to make it plural.

| one wolf | two wolves | one knife | two knives |

1 **Complete each sentence with the correct plural.**

1 There were some ___wolves___ (wolf)  in the mountains.

2 The books are on the ___shelfes___ (shelf)

3 The ___knives___ (knife) were very sharp.

4 I cut the apple into two ___halfes___ (half)  .

Grammar

Do you remember about animals in the Gobi desert?

A camel is as strong as a yak.
A gazelle is faster than a snow leopard.

1 Ask and answer.

camel – strong – yak
camel – fast – gazelle

Is a camel as strong as a yak?

Yes, it is.

Is a camel as fast as a gazelle?

No, it isn't.

You can also answer:
I don't know!

1 yak – fast – snow leopard
3 zebra – tall – camel
5 lion – fierce – snow leopard

2 gazelle – strong – camel
4 gazelle – big – yak
6 goat – heavy – sheep

**2 Compare the animals. Say. Then write.
The words in the box can help you.**

Remember! Add -er

| strong | slow | fast | big | small | tall |

A camel is stronger than a goat.

1      strong   stronger   2   taller

3   tall   slower   4   tall   er

5   Biger   faster   6   faster

**3 Compare you and your friend.
Say. Then write.**

Who is taller?   Who is shorter?   Whose hair is longer?
Whose hair is darker?

Listening

Two brothers ...
different lives ...

1 These two men are brothers. One is called Batold and one is called Avir.
Listen and write the correct name.

_____   _____

2 Look at the statements below.
Listen and circle true (T) or false (F).

1 Avir's house was bigger than Batold's.	T	F
2 Batold's family was smaller than Avir's.	T	F
3 The brothers had five children all together.	T	F
4 Avir's children were older than Batold's.	T	F
5 Avir was not as rich as Batold.	T	F
6 Avir was as happy as Batold.	T	F

3 Listen and sing.

White Sheep and Black Sheep
White sheep and black sheep,
   Graze on a hill.
When the wind stops
   You all stand still.
When the wind blows
   You walk away slow.
White sheep and black sheep,
   Where do you go? *Terry Kluytmans*

Listening focus   *identifying characters; listening for detail*

Spelling

 The letter **y** on the end of some nouns says **ee**.

A new **baby** gazelle cannot walk at all.

1 **Say the sounds. Make the words.**

1 pupp → y
puppy

2 jell → y
jelly

3 lad → y
lady

4 stor → y
story

5 tedd → y
teddy

6 lorr → y
lorry

2 **Write.**

1
The _lady_ has a _buybdy_ .

2
The _puppy_ is sleeping.

3
This _story_ is about a _lo pages_ .

4
The _lady_ is driving a _van_ .

5
I like to eat _Jeli_ .

6
The _pupy_ is eating the _Jell_ .

3 **Tick ✓ the words you can read.**

puppy ☐ jelly ☐ lady ☐ story ☑ teddy ☐ lorry ☐

Spelling focus **y** *saying* **e**

Class writing

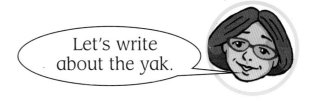

Let's write about the yak.

1 **Read the labels. Write them on the picture.**

| long hair |
| soft woolly hair underneath |
| horns |

| hooves | 700 kg |
| 190 cms |

long ha
horns
soft wolly hair under neath
hooves
700 kg
190 cm

2 **Look at the picture. What does it tell you about yaks? Write a description.**

The horse race 🎧

'Watch me, father!' Shirav called. He leapt onto his horse and disappeared in a cloud of dust. Sukhe stood quietly beside his father. His father's eyes were fixed on the massive rock at the far side of the valley. Proudly, he watched Shirav ride around it and start back towards them. Shirav was the fastest rider in the valley. Perhaps he was the fastest in the whole desert!

'Did I do well, father?' asked Shirav as he jumped down from his horse.

'You did very well, Shirav,' replied his father. 'You are a good rider.'

Shirav smiled. 'I can't wait for tomorrow!' he said.

The next morning everyone got up early. It was festival day at last! There were games and horse races on festival day. Sukhe and his family set off towards the next valley. Shirav and his father rode their horses. Sukhe drove the cart. His mother and grandmother sat behind him. They laughed and sang happily.

    Parents: *see extra material on page 166*

When they got to the next valley, friends waved to them and called out greetings.

The boys' race was first. Sukhe took his horse from the cart.

'Just do your best,' his father said. He helped Sukhe onto the horse. 'You are only eight years old and this is your first race. Remember, Shirav is thirteen – and he won this race last year! Now go and join the other boys at the start.' He pointed to a crowd of young riders beside a blue and red flag.

Sukhe rode to the flag. His horse snorted with excitement. The other horses stamped their hooves and tossed their heads. Then, they were off! Sukhe held on tightly as he raced along the valley. There were many riders in front of Sukhe but his horse was fast. Little by little, Sukhe came nearer to the leaders. When they turned to go back, there were only ten riders in front. Sukhe's horse galloped strongly. He passed several riders. Then he saw Shirav's blue and green coat ahead of him.

'Run! Run!' Sukhe told his horse. 'You are the strongest!' At the sound of his voice, the horse leapt forwards. Shirav and Sukhe passed the leaders. The flag was not far away. Sukhe looked across at Shirav. His brother's eyes were fixed on the flag. He really wanted to win. Sukhe knew then that it was Shirav's race. Sukhe passed the flag just a moment after Shirav.

'I did my best,' Sukhe told his father.

'Sukhe,' said his father, 'I have two winners today. I am the proudest man in the world!'

Reading and understanding

1 **Answer the questions. Write the names.**

1 Who is the fastest rider in the valley? _Shiver_ ~~rave~~

2 Who drove the cart to the next valley? _sukhe_

3 Who laughed and sang happily? _fathe , mather_

4 Who won the race last year? _shirave_

5 Who won this race? _shirave_

6 Who came second? _sukhe_

7 Who is the proudest man in the world? _Sukhe father_

2 **Discuss the best ending for these sentences. Tick ✓ the box.**

1 Sukhe's mother and grandmother were happy because
   a they were in the cart. [✓]   b it was festival day. [ ]
   c they could sing. [ ]

2 The blue and red flag marked
   a the start of the race. [ ]   b the finish of the race. [✓]
   c the start and the finish of the race. [ ]

3 Shirav's eyes were fixed on the flag because he wanted to
   a get to the flag. [✓]   b pass the flag first. [ ]
   c finish the race. [ ]

4 Sukhe's father was the proudest man in the world because
   a Sukhe came second. [ ]   b Shirav won the race. [ ]
   c his sons came first and second. [✓]

Get active 5

Working with words

 Complete the sentences.

| snorted   galloped   stamped |
| leaped   tossed its head |

1 The horse ran very fast. It _galloped_ .

2 The horse moved its head up and down. It _tossed it's head_

3 The horse put its feet down hard on the ground. It _stamped_ .

4 The horse jumped forwards. It _leaped_ .

5 The horse blew air through its nose. It _snorted_ .

Sentence building

*Remember! We must put a **punctuation mark** at the end of a sentence.*

This is my horse.

Do you like my horse?

Look at me!

| Most sentences end with a **full stop**. | We put a **question mark** at the end of a question. | We use an **exclamation mark** if we say something **loudly**, or if we are **surprised**. |

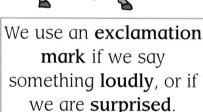

 What punctuation mark goes at the end of each sentence?

1
Run faster !

2
My horse is white .

3
Who are you ?

4
Can you ride a horse ?

5
Stop !

6
The sun is shining .

Grammar

> Do you remember the story about the horse race?

Shirav was the fastest rider in the valley.

Sukhe's horse was the strongest in the race.

'I am the proudest man in the world.'

1 **Circle the correct words.**

1 Shirav was **the slowest** **the fastest** rider in the whole desert.
2 The boys' grandmother was **the oldest** **the youngest** in the family.
3 **Sukhe**, **Shirav** was the youngest in the family.
4 Sukhe's horse was **the strongest** **the weakest** in the race.
5 Sukhe's **uncle** **father** was the proudest man in the world.

2 **Finish the sentences. Use the words in the box.**

young strong fast proud	Remember! Add **-est**

1 Sukhe's father was the ___Proudest___ man in the world.
2 Shirav was the ___fastest___ rider in the whole desert.
3 Sukhe was the ___youngest___ in the family.
4 Sukhe's horse was the ___strongest___ in the race.

3 **Think about your family.**

Who is the oldest in your family? Who is the youngest?
Who is the tallest? Who is the shortest?
Who is the prettiest? Who is the noisiest?
Who is the cleverest?
Now ask and answer with a friend.

Listening

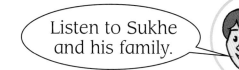

Listen to Sukhe and his family.

1 Look at these people.
Who are they? What do you know about them?

2 Listen to the family at the horse race. Who is speaking?
Write the names.

1 _____   2 _____

_____   _____

3 _____   4 _____

_____   _____

5 _____

_____

3 Listen again.
Were they speaking before the race, during the race or after the race? Write *Before*, *During* or *After* under each name above.

4 Listen and sing.

Trot, trot, trot,
Go and never stop,
I can ride my little pony,
Though the way is rough and stony,
Go and never stop,
Trot, trot, trot, trot, trot.

Spelling

The letters **oi** in some words sounds like **oy**.

At the sound of his **voice**, the horse leapt forward.

1 Listen and read.

The oil will spoil if you boil it.

Write the words in the sentence which sound the same as **oil**.

spoil   _boil_

2 Say the sounds. Write the words.

1 c → oi → n   2 j → oi → n   3 n → oi → se   4 s → oi → l

coin   _Join_   _noise_   _soil_

3 Solve the clues with words from the box.

| join   soil   voice   noise   coin |

1 We grow plants in this. _soil_

2 money _coin_

3 We use this for speaking and singing. _horse_

4 fit together _join_

5 sounds _voice_

4 Tick ✓ the words you can read.

coin ✓   oil ✓   noise ✓   voice ✓   join ✓   boil ✓   soil ✓   spoil ✓

Class writing

Let's write a story.

1 **Read and look at the pictures.**

In winter it snows in the Gobi desert. One day Sukhe and Shirav played in the snow. Look at what happened.

2 **Read these openings for the story.**
Which opening is the most interesting? Why?

1 There was snow on the ground.

2 Shirav and Sukhe looked at the snow.

3 'Look at the snow!' said Shirav.

Choose a beginning. Continue the story.

22nd March 11

Ice age giants 🎧

A long time ago the world was colder than it is today. There was a lot of ice and snow. People made their homes in caves. They kept warm inside. Many giant animals lived at that time.

The woolly mammoth was the most enormous animal on land. It was as big as a lorry. It had long curved tusks and a thick coat. Mammoths lived in huge herds. They ate grass and leaves. The last mammoths died 11,000 years ago.

 Mammoths were bigger than elephants. Today, elephants live in warm places in Africa and India. They do not have thick coats of hair. They do not need hair on their skins because the sun keeps them warm.

This giant sloth was as big as a bus. It walked on two legs and it ate leaves from the tops of trees. It had long fur and three sharp claws in its paws. Beneath its skin it had flat pieces of hard bone. Other animals did not attack it.

Sloths are living today in South America. They hang upside down in the rainforest. They crawl slowly along the branches. This sloth is much smaller than the giant sloth.

mammoth   elephant   giant sloth   sloth   giant bear   bear

 Parents: see extra material on page 166

This animal was as big as a family car. Its body was covered with hard scales. Other animals could not attack it. Its tail was made of bone. At the end were sharp spikes. It could use its tail to hit other animals.

A smaller animal like this one is living today.
It lives in South America. It is an armadillo.
It has hard scales on its back. It does not have
a tail with spikes. It rolls up into a ball.
It is more difficult for other animals to attack it.

This animal was as big as a small car. It had two very long curved teeth. They were as sharp as knives. It is called the sabre-tooth cat. A sabre is a curved knife. This animal used its teeth to kill quickly.

Lions, tigers and leopards are big cats. They are all a little smaller than the sabre-tooth cat but they hunt in the same way. They look for an old or sick animal. They chase it away from the herd. Then they have a better chance of catching it.

glyptodont   armadillo   woolly rhino   rhino   sabre-tooth cat   lion

Reading and understanding

1 **Complete the sentences.**

1 The biggest animal on land was the _____ .

2 Elephants do not have thick _____ because the sun keeps them warm.

3 The giant sloth ate _____ .

4 The glyptodont's tail was made of _____ .

5 There were _____ at the end of the glyptodont's tail.

6 The armadillo lives in _____ .

7 A sabre is a curved _____ .

2 **Name the animals.**

1 It rolls itself into a ball. _____

2 It hangs upside down in trees. _____

3 It had two long curved teeth. _____

4 They hunt old or sick animals. _____

5 It had flat pieces of hard bone under its skin. _____

3 **Write the names. Match.**

1 _____ 2 _____ 3 _____ 4 _____

a b c d

Get active 6

Working with words

1 **Write the words.**

fur	bone	claw	wool	knife
	scale	spike	tusk	hair

1 Find three things that are sharp. ——————— ——————— ———————

2 Find three things that are soft. ——————— ——————— ———————

3 Find three things that are hard. ——————— ——————— ———————

Sentence building

Remember! A **verb** is a **doing** word.

The **past tense** of many verbs end in **ed**.
These are called **regular** verbs.

People **hunted** woolly mammoths with spears.
verb – hunt   past tense – hunted

The **past tense** of some verbs do not end in **ed**.
These are called **irregular** verbs.

Woolly mammoths **ate** grass and leaves.
verb – eat   past tense – ate

1 **Match up each verb with its past tense.**

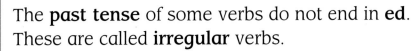

1	sleep	a	caught
2	write	b	flew
3	catch	c	slept
4	swim	d	saw
5	fly	e	swam
6	see	f	wrote

2 **Make up some sentences. Use the verbs above.**

Grammar

Do you remember the ice age giants?

The woolly rhino was **dangerous**.

The mammoth was **more dangerous**.

The sabre-tooth cat was **the most dangerous**.

1 **Ask and answer.**

cat
Dangerous   A   B

Which cat is more dangerous?

1 bear
   frightening   A   B

2 bird
   beautiful   A   B

2 **Look and say.**
beautiful

A   B   C

I think C is the most beautiful.

1 delicious   A   B   C

2 frightening   A   B   C

3 **Look at this!**

A   B   C

A is good. B is better. C is the best.

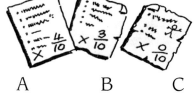
A   B   C

A is bad. B is worse. C is the worst.

4 **Now you!**

1

2

Listening

What amazing animals!

1 Listen. What do you know about these animals?

1 blue whale

2 peacock

_____

_____

3 box jellyfish

4 platypus

_____

_____

5 polar bear

6 dolphin

_____

_____

2 Look at these adjectives.
Listen again and write an adjective under each photo.

> extraordinary   beautiful   enormous
> poisonous   dangerous   intelligent

3 Talk about the animals.

4 Listen and sing.

Brown bear's snoring, brown bear's snoring,
In his winter sleep.
Brown bear's snoring, brown bear's snoring,
In his winter sleep.
But snow and ice are melting,
Icicles are dropping,
Brown bear's ears are listening
And his eyes begin to peep.

Spelling

 The letters **aw** in words makes a sound like **or**.

Sloths **crawl** slowly along branches.

1 Add *aw* to finish each word. Read the words you have made. Discuss the meaning of each word.

1  j — —

2  p — —

3   cl — —

4  dr — —

2 Write the rhyming words from the box.

yawn  shawl  paw

1 Saw rhymes with _____ .
2 Dawn rhymes with _____ .
3 Crawl rhymes with _____ .

3 Choose three *aw* words from this page. Make up a sentence about each word.

I like to dr**aw**.

4 Tick ✓ the words you can read.

saw ☐   dawn ☐   claw ☐   crawl ☐   paw ☐   yawn ☐
☐ draw ☐ shawl ☐ jaw ☐

Class writing

Let's write about the woolly rhino.

1 How big was the woolly rhino?

2 What did the woolly rhino look like? What did it eat? Where did it live?

3 Where do rhinos live now? How big are they? What do they look like?

Writing focus   *factual information*

59

Revision 2
You can do it!

1 **Look at the pictures.**
Which animals do you like? Why?
Which animals don't you like? Why?

2 **Listen and read.**

3 **Read and say.**

1 What animal hunts monkeys?
2 What is the fastest of these animals?
3 Where do monkeys sleep?
4 Which are the strongest parts of a crocodile?
5 How tall is a giraffe?
6 Which of these animals are hunters?
7 Which animals can hide well?
8 How does a crocodile hide?
9 What does a giraffe eat?

The children learned about animals in Africa. They wrote about them.

> Tilly, please tell us about giraffes.

> They are the tallest animals in the world. They can be five metres tall. They are big but they can run at 56 kph. That is nearly as fast as a lion.

> Ben, what did you write about lions?

> Lionesses are better hunters than lions. They hunt together and they can run at 50–60 kph. They do not hunt every day. Lions protect the lionesses and the cubs.

Sam, what can you say about leopards?

They are good climbers. They hunt at night and they climb trees quietly. They catch monkeys and other animals when they are sleeping in the branches.

Nina, please tell us about crocodiles.

Crocodiles are the best hunters in the rivers. They have strong mouths with lots of teeth. They have strong tails, too. They hit animals into the water with their tails.

4 Listen and find the picture.

5 Think of an animal that is:
more frightening than a crocodile
prettier than a lion cub
more beautiful than a giraffe
a better climber than a leopard.

6 Act out the story.

7 Write the words.

_____   _____

_____   _____

_____   _____

Flight

Birds in the air

In the sun's bright glare,
the earth glows red,
birds fly through the air
above my head.

Over tall green trees,
a flock of sheep,
and turquoise seas,
where dolphins leap.

They're going to see
the mountain snow.
They're going to be
Where cool rivers flow.

I want to fly
where they fly, too,
rising high
in skies of blue.

I want to go
where clouds float by,
I want to know
what it's like to fly.

Parents: *see extra material on page 166*

Did you see it?

Did you see the duck?
Did you see the sheep?
Did you see the old red rooster
perching half asleep?

Did you see the fire
under the balloon?
Did you see it rise up
like a huge blue moon?

Did you see it drop
gently to the ground?
Did you hear the cheer
from everyone around?

It was so exciting,
I can't believe it's true,
The animals went flying,
Did you see it, too?

Reading and understanding

1 **Answer the questions.**

Poem 1: Birds in the air

1 What colour is the earth? _____

2 What things do the birds fly over? _____

_____

3 What are the birds going to see? _____

4 What does the boy want to do? _____

Poem 2: Did you see it?

5 Which animals are in the poem? _____

_____

6 What was under the balloon? _____

7 What did the balloon look like? _____

8 What did the people do when the balloon came down again?

_____

2 **Read the poems again. Find the answers to these questions.**

Poem 1: Birds in the air

1 Is the sun shining strongly? Which words tell you?
2 Are the birds going to fly far? How do you know?
3 Do you think the boy is feeling hot? How do you know?

Poem 2: Did you see it?

4 Was the rooster frightened? How do you know?
5 Did the balloon go up and down quickly or slowly?
   Which words tell you?
6 Did people like the balloon? How do you know?

Get active 7

Comprehension focus *Consolidation of new language in* Flight

Working with words

1 Match the words from the poem with the objects in the poem. Write the words.

glows   flows   leap   float

1 _____ 2 _____ 3 _____ 4 _____

2 Find thc words.

1 Which word means to stay high or on top? _____

2 Which word means to jump high? _____

3 Which word means to shine but not brightly? _____

4 Which word means to move along gently? _____

Sentence building

A *collective noun* is a **group of people or things**.

There is a **flock** of sheep in the field.

1 Match the phrases with the pictures.

a a swarm of bees ☐   b a herd of cows ☐   c a bunch of flowers ☐
d a class of children ☐   e a team of footballers ☐   f a library of books ☐

1  2   3  4  5   6

2 Which is the collective noun in each phrase?

Grammar

Do you remember the poems about flying?

What **is going to** happen?

The birds **are going to** fly over the snow.

The balloon **is going to** rise up into the sky.

1 Finish the sentences.

1 The plane is going to ...   a leap out of the water.

2 The helicopter is going to ...   b dive into the sea.

3 The penguins are going to ...   c fly away.

4 The dolphin is going to ...   d take off.

5 The birds are going to ...   e land.

2 What are you going to do tomorrow? Write Y (yes) or N (no).

come to school ☐   watch TV ☐

help your mum and dad ☐   play with your friends ☐

go to the sports club ☐   do your homework ☐

Ask and answer.
Are you going to come to school tomorrow? Yes, I am. or No, I'm not.

3 Answer the questions. Say. Then write.

1 What are you going to do next weekend? _I am going to_____.

2 What are you going to do next holidays? _____.

Listening

Listen to Lucy and her dad.

Next week Lucy's family is going to travel to Coconut Island for a holiday.

Her father is talking to her about their plans and they are looking at a map.

1 Listen and point to the places on the map.

Dolphin point

Jamestown

Sandy Bay

2 Listen again. Then answer these questions.

1 Where are Lucy and her family going to stay?
2 What are they going to do? Name three things.
3 What are they going to see? How many things can you name?
4 Do you think it is going to be a good holiday?

3 Listen and sing.

Lazy coconut tree

Some folk like to go fishing
Far across the bay.
I would rather be dreaming
On the beach all day.

Like the lazy co-co-coconut,
    co-co-coconut tree,
Like the lazy co-co-coconut,
    co-co-coconut tree.

John Emlyn Edwards

Spelling

The letters **air** and **are** can make the same sound.

In the Sun's bright **glare**,
the earth glows red,
birds fly through the **air**
above my head.

1 Add *air* to finish these words. Read the words. Write the words.

1 ch _air_

chair

2 p _____

_____

3 st _____ s

_____

2 Finish these words with *are*. Read the words. Write the words.

1 squ _____

_____

2 h _____

_____

3 st _____

_____

3 Use each word in a sentence of your own.

1 hair _____

2 hare _____

3 stairs _____

4 stare _____

4 Tick ✓ the words you can read.

chair ☐ square ☐ hair ☐ hare ☐ stairs ☐ stare ☐

Class writing

Let's finish the poems.

1 **Look at the picture. Read and choose words.**

Pink and orange,
blue and red,
a cloud of colours
above my _____ .

| floor   bed   head |
| wall   room |

Purple and yellow
white and _____
How many are there?
There are _____ .

| blue   three   green   more |
| two   fourteen   red |

2 **Find words and write.**

1 Find another pair of rhyming words in the box. Write them.
_____ _____

2 Look at the picture and the colous. Use rhyming
  words to help you finish the poem.

These are my balloons,
__Green__ and _____ .
How many have I got?
I've got _____ .

Holiday island

Anna, Pete, Tim and Sue are on holiday on a small island. On their first morning, their father is taking them for a walk. They are exploring the beach.

Pete:	Look! Here's a cave!
Sue:	Wow! It's really dark in there. I can't see the back of it.
Anna:	Can we look inside, Dad?
Dad:	Let's all go in. But you must be careful.
Tim:	Why? Are there pirates in there?
Pete:	Don't be silly, Tim!
Dad:	Of course there aren't any pirates! But you mustn't climb on the rocks. They are wet and you can easily fall.
Anna:	Come on, everyone. Let's find something interesting.
Sue:	It smells strange in here.
Dad:	It's the seaweed.
Pete:	It's chilly, isn't it?
Tim:	That's because there's water dripping down the walls.
Sue:	The rocks are rough, and there are tiny shells on them.
Dad:	Be careful, they're sharp.
Pete:	Look at this seashell. It's as big as my hand.
Sue:	It has a lovely curly pattern. It's really pretty.
Anna:	This shell has spikes. Look, it's smooth and pink inside.
Tim:	Mine is curly and it's pointed at the top.
Sue:	I've got this shell. It's flat and it looks like a little fan.
Dad:	Well, look at this. It has spots!

Parents: *see extra material on page 166*

Anna:	What's making that noise?
Tim:	It sounds like water splashing.
Pete:	I can hear it, too. Is there a little stream somewhere?
Tim:	Yes, there it is. It's running out from under that rock.
Sue:	Let's go and see.
Dad:	You mustn't go past the rock.
Tim:	Alright, Dad. Look here. There's a pool.
Sue:	Great! I'm going to look for a crab.
Anna:	Perhaps there's one under that stone. Turn it over.
Sue:	Ouch! The water's icy. Oh, Look!
Pete:	Is it a crab?
Sue:	No. It's treasure! A gold necklace.
Tim:	And it has jewels!
Pete:	Dad! See what we've got.
Dad:	It's very beautiful.
Anna:	Can we keep it?
Dad:	No, of course not. We must take it to the police.
Pete:	Do we have to?
Dad:	Yes, we do. This necklace is valuable. It belongs to someone. The police can find out who lost it.

Reading and understanding

1   **Read and circle true (T) or false (F).**

1	The children must not touch the rocks in the cave.	T	F
2	It smells sweet in the cave.	T	F
3	The curly shell is as big as Pete's hand.	T	F
4	Anna hears fish splashing.	T	F
5	The stream is coming from under a rock.	T	F
6	Sue wants to look for treasure.	T	F
7	She says 'Ouch!' because the water is very cold.	T	F
8	There is a crab under the stone.	T	F
9	The necklace has jewels in it.	T	F
10	The children must keep the necklace.	T	F

2   **Discuss your ideas.**

Why was the necklace under the stone?

1 Did someone lose it on the beach?

2 Did the sea carry the necklace into the cave?

3 Did someone hide it under the stone?

4 Did someone leave it in the cave?

5 Was the necklace under the stone for a long time?
Was it only there for a short time?

Get active   8

Working with words

1 Who found these shells? Write the names.

1 _____ 2 _____ 3 _____ 4 _____ 5 _____

2 Find the opposites of these words.

1 warm _____ 2 light _____ 3 ugly _____

4 dry _____ 5 smooth _____ 6 enormous _____

Sentence building

*Discuss how the spelling of the two verbs below change when we add **ing** to them.*

*Remember! The spelling of some verbs change when we add **ing**.*

We hop.
We are **hopping**.
hop + ing = hopping

I take the children for a walk.
I am **taking** the children for a walk.
take + ing = taking

1 Write the underlined verb in two ways.

1 We are <u>exploring</u> the beach. <u>explore</u> <u>exploring</u>

2 I am <u>running</u> fast. _____ _____

3 The dog is <u>wagging</u> its tail. _____ _____

4 I was <u>waving</u> to my friend. _____ _____

5 The children are <u>swimming</u>. _____ _____

6 The lady is <u>closing</u> the door. _____ _____

Grammar

Do you remember holiday island?

You **must** be careful!
You **mustn't** climb on the rocks.
You **mustn't** go into the cave alone.
We **must** take the necklace to the police.

1 What must you do on the beach when it is very hot and sunny?
We must ...

1 wear   2 drink    3 wear

4 sit   5 put on

2 Look at these signs. What mustn't you do?
You mustn't ...

1   2 **Keep off the grass**   3

4 **No Ball Games**   5 **Quiet please**

3 What are the rules of your class?
What must you do? What mustn't you do?
Talk about it. Then write.

| Remember! |
| mustn't = must not |

Class rules

We must _____
_____

We must not _____
_____

Listening

Listen to the children and their dad.

Do you remember Anna, Pete, Tim and Sue? They went to the beach with their father. What did they find? Where did they find it? Do you remember?

1 Listen. Then answer these questions.

1 Where are the children going today?
2 Are they all happy about this?
3 What must they do before they leave?

2 Listen. Tick ✓ the things they must take with them.

sunglasses ☐	water ☐
swimming costumes ☐	sandwiches ☐
towels ☐	ice creams ☐
shorts ☐	fruit ☐
sunhats ☐	a map ☐
sun cream ☐	a torch ☐

3 Listen and say.

sun on the sand sun on the sea sun on the sailing boats sun on me

Spelling

The letters **ew** can say **oo** in some words.

It's treasure!

And it has **jewels**.

1 Add *ew* to make these past tense verbs.

		Today	Yesterday
1	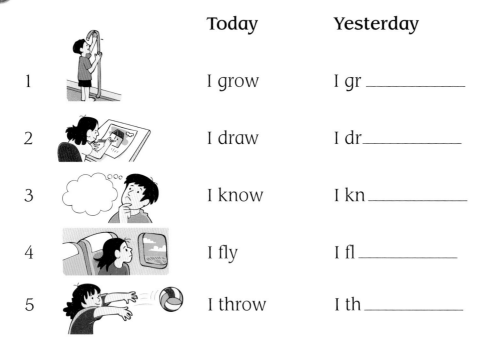	I grow	I gr _____
2		I draw	I dr _____
3		I know	I kn _____
4		I fly	I fl _____
5		I throw	I th _____

2 Use the words you have made to finish these sentences.

1 The bird _____ in the sky.

2 The tree _____ very tall.

3 I _____ the answer to the question.

4 She _____ the ball up into the air.

3 Tick ✓ the words you can read.

grew ☐   drew ☐   knew ☐   flew ☐   threw ☐

Class writing

Let's write the ending of the play.

1 **Dad and the children went to the police station.**
Complete the dialogue.

Policeman: Good morning. Can I help you?

Dad: _____

Policeman: Where did you find it?

Anna: _____

Policeman: Did you see anybody else on the beach?

Tim: _____

Policeman: Do you live on the island?

Pete: _____

Policeman: Well, a lady lost a necklace. I think this is hers.

2 **Which lady lost the necklace? When? How? Finish the dialogue.**

Mrs Green

Mrs Strong

Mrs Bell

Dad: Who lost the necklace?

Policeman: _____

Pete: When did she lose it?

Policeman: _____

Tim   How did she lose it?

Policeman: _____

Sue: Can we give it back to her?

Policeman: _____

Anna: Is she going to be pleased?

Policeman: _____

A letter from a sailor

sail

hammock

mast

My dear Harry,

At last I have time to write to you. I am having the most exciting adventures!

Now we are sailing through sparkling blue seas. The sun shines every day and the wind is gentle. It is blowing us towards India. Last week it was not like this.

One evening the sky suddenly grew dark. The sun disappeared behind black clouds. We saw a flash of lightning and we heard the rumble of thunder. The wind grew stronger. Quickly, the captain gave orders. We lowered the biggest sail. Then the storm hit us. The waves got higher and threw the ship up and down. The rain fell heavily. Our clothes were soaked with rain and sea water. We got another sail down. Then the wind ripped the last sail. It flapped around the mast in two pieces. Suddenly, the wind tore them away. They flew off into the darkness. After that, we all went below. It was the most frightening night of my life. I could not sleep at all. My hammock swung backwards and forwards. I felt terrible.

Captain

deck

When the sun came up, the sky was blue and there was almost no wind. We sailed slowly to the nearest port. It was a very busy place. I saw wonderful things and I ate some delicious food. In the market there were baskets full of fruit. I liked the oranges best. There were some very strange fish. One was bright red. It had spines on its back and a huge blue mouth. I wanted to touch the spines. The fish seller stopped me.

'Those spines are dangerous,' he said.

'Why?' I asked.

'Because they have poison in them,' he told me. Of course, I did not touch that fish.

We stayed in the port for three days. We put up a new sail and tidied the deck. We are going to arrive in India in a few days. I want to ride on an elephant. My friend Jim says they are the biggest animals in the world. He saw elephants in Africa. They were as tall as the trees.

I hope you are working hard in school. Are you learning a lot of new things? You can write to me. I want to know what you are doing.

Your cousin, Tom

Reading and understanding

1 **Answer these questions. Write the names.**

1 Who wrote the letter? _____

2 Who is the letter to? _____

3 Who gave the orders on the ship? _____

4 Who was frightened of the storm? _____

5 Who said, 'Those spines are dangerous.'? _____

6 Who is Tom's friend? _____

7 Who is Tom's cousin? _____

2 **Discuss the best ending for these sentences. Tick ✓ the box.**

1 The sailors took the sails down because

a there was thunder. ☐   b the wind was too strong. ☐

c they saw lightning. ☐

2 Tom could not sleep on the night of the storm because

a he was frightened. ☐   b he was wet. ☐   c he was cold. ☐

3 Tom did not touch the red fish because

a it had spikes. ☐   b it was dangerous. ☐

c it was poisonous. ☐

3 **Answer these questions.**

1 Does Tom like being a sailor? How do you know?
2 Who has been to Africa? What did he see there?
3 Is Harry younger than Tom? How do you know?

Get active 9

Working with words

1 **Match the pictures with the words.**

1 delicious _____   2 sparkling _____   3 strange _____

4 dangerous _____   5 busy _____

2 **Write the word.**

1 a lot of things happening _____   2 unusual _____

3 shining brightly _____   4 can hurt _____

5 tasting very good _____

Sentence building

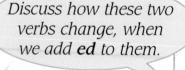

Discuss how these two verbs change, when we add **ed** to them.

The wind **ripped** the sail.
rip + ed = ripped

The captain **smiled** at me.
smile + ed = smiled

Remember! The spelling of some verbs change when we add **ed**.

1 **Add *ed* to each verb.**
Spell each verb correctly!

1 stop _stopped_   2 like _____
3 drop _____   4 wave _____
5 hop   _____   6 close _____
7 tap   _____   8 skate _____
9 slip _____   10 use   _____

2 **Make up some sentences. Use each *ed* verb in them.**

Grammar

Do you remember Tom the sailor?

Tom **wanted to touch** the spines.
The spines were dangerous.
Why were they dangerous**?**
The spines were dangerous **because** they had poison in them.

1 **Finish the sentences.**

1 The sky grew dark ...

2 They lowered the big sail ...

3 Their clothes were soaked ...

4 Tom did not sleep ...

a because his hammock was swinging about.

b because the sun went behind the clouds.

c because the wind was so strong.

d because the rain was so heavy.

2 **Ask and answer.**

Was Tom frightened during the storm?   Yes, he was.

Why?   Because the ship went up and down.

1 Was Tom happy after the storm?
3 Did Tom go to the market?
5 Did they stay in the port for a few days?

2 Did Tom like the port?
4 Did Tom like the oranges best?
6 Did Tom want to go to India?

3 **What did Tom want to do in India?**

He wanted to ride an elephant.

1    2    3    4

Listening

Here's a
funny story.

1 When Tom came home from sea, he told Harry lots of stories about his adventures in India. Look at the pictures and listen to Tom's story.

2 Can you tell the story?

3 Listen and sing.

See the monkey at the zoo.
Monkey see, monkey do.
Clap your hands, he does too.
Monkey see, monkey do.

Stamp you feet … Wave your arms … Turn around …

Spelling

In **wh** words sometimes you can't hear the **h**.

When the sun came up, the sky was blue.

1 Add *wh* to finish these words. Read the words. Write the words.

1

_____ eel

_____

2

_____ iskers

_____

3

_____ ale

_____

4

_____ isper

_____

2 Write the question words.

wh
- en _____
- at _____
- y _____
- ere _____
- ich _____

3 Make up a sentence beginning with each *wh* question word.

4 Tick ✓ the words you can read.

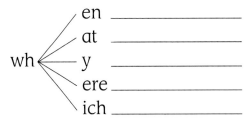

wheel ☐   when ☐   whiskers ☐   what ☐   whale ☐

why ☐   whisper ☐   which ☐

Class writing

Let's write a letter.

Harry is writing to Tom. He is telling Tom what he did last week. Look at the pictures. Finish his letter.

Dear Tom

   Thank you for your letter. The storm was exciting but it was dangerous! I am glad that you are safe and well.

   I worked very hard last week. We learned about ...

_____

_____

_____

_____

_____

_____

_____

Revision 3
You can do it!

1 **Look at the pictures.**
Do you go to school by bus or car?
Do you want to fly in a plane? Why?
Where do you want to go?
Do you want to sail in a boat? Why or why not?

2 **Listen and read.**

3 **Read and say.**
1 Why must Tom fasten his seat belt?
2 Why must Billy sit down?
3 Why must Joe wear a life jacket?
4 Why can't Anna's mum look at her picture?
5 What is Tom going to do on the plane?
6 What can Billy see in the sky?
7 What are Joe and his dad going to do?
8 What did Anna draw?

I don't want to wear that, dad.

You must wear a life jacket, Joe. The water is deep.

Look at my picture, mum.

I can't look at it, Anna. I have to look at the road.

4 Listen and say which picture. 🎧

5 Listen again and answer the questions. 🎧

1 Who is going to be late?
2 Who is going to go to London?
3 Who is going to sail to an island?
4 Who is going to see another helicopter?

6 Act out the story.

7 Write the words.

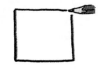

_____   _____

_____   _____

_____   _____

Pictures 🎧

People like to have pictures of their families and friends. They have pictures of places they visit and things they like, too. They can get these pictures easily. It was not always like this.

The first people made pictures inside caves. They made colours from earth and rocks. They painted pictures of men and animals. They lit torches in caves. The torches gave them light. Then they could see when they were painting. Some cave paintings are 30,000 years old.

The tombs of the pharaohs had many paintings on the walls. The paintings told the story of the pharaoh's life. These paintings are 3,000 years old. Later, people painted on walls in cities and towns. The pictures often told the story of something important. The paintings were for everyone to look at.

Rich people wanted to have pictures in their homes. Artists painted pictures of their families and their favourite things. Poor people did not have pictures of anything. Only rich people could pay the artists. The paintings were expensive because they took a long time to do.

Parents: see extra material on page 166

About 200 years ago a few people made pictures with cameras. The pictures were not very good and they were not in colour. Slowly, the pictures got better. These were the first photographs. People liked them because the photographers could make them quickly. They could make cheap copies, too, and more people could buy them. They bought photographs of other countries. They found out about different people. Newspapers had photographs and people saw pictures of what was happening all over the world.

Photographs and cameras got even better. Lots of people bought their own cameras. They took pictures in colour. They took pictures of their families, their friends and their holidays.

Now people take pictures with a digital camera. People download these pictures onto their computers. They email them to friends all over the world. Some people take pictures with their mobile phones. A person could take a picture of a cave painting with a mobile phone. Then he could send it to a friend's phone in just a few seconds.

Reading and understanding

1 **Answer the questions.**

1 Where did the first people make pictures?
_____

2 What did they paint pictures of?
_____

3 Where were the paintings of pharaohs?
_____

4 What story did they tell?
_____

5 Why were paintings expensive?
_____

6 What can people use to take pictures with now?
_____

7 How long does it take to send a picture from a mobile phone?
_____

2 **Discuss answers to these questions.**

1 Why did poor people not have paintings in their houses?
2 Why were photographs cheaper than paintings?
3 Why could more people buy copies of photographs?
4 Why did people want to buy their own cameras?
5 Are photographs cheaper than paintings today?

3 **Which came first? Order the pictures.**

a   b   c   d

Get active 10

e   f

Working with words

1 Match the opposite meanings. Write the pairs of words.

easy	worse	same	expensive
different	cheap	last	poor
first	rich	better	difficult

1 _____   2 _____   3 _____

_____   _____   _____

4 _____   5 _____   6 _____

_____   _____   _____

Sentence building

> Remember! An **adverb** tells us more about a **verb**. An **adverb of manner** answers the question **how**? Most adverbs of manner end with **ly**

How did the man paint the picture?
The man painted the picture **quickly**.
quick + ly = quickly

How did the children shout?
The children shouted **noisily**.

noisy + ly = noisily

> Notice the way the spelling changes with this word.

1 Spell the adverbs correctly.

1 slow + ly = _____   2 quiet + ly = _____

3 sweet + ly = _____   4 angry + ly = _____

5 happy + ly = _____   6 easy + ly = _____

2 Make up some sentences. Use each adverb of manner above in them.

Grammar

Do you remember?

Torches helped cave people to see when they were painting.

Newspapers started to have photographs. People saw what was happening all over the world.

1 What were the people doing when the photographer took the pictures?
These words can help you.

| play   open   eat   jump |

1

The girl was playing the piano.

2

3

4

5

6

2 Cover the photos. Can you remember them? Ask and answer.

| woman   men   dolphin   girl   boy   men |

boy

What was the boy doing?

He was playing a computer game.

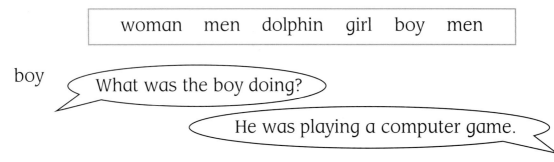

Listening

Poor Matthew!

Matthew Stevens is a chef at a restaurant. Something extraordinary happened to him one day in April, 2005.

1 Cover the pictures below and listen to Matthew's story.

2 Answer these questions.

What bit him? A dog? A horse? A spider?
What saved him? His friend? His computer? His mobile phone?

3 Look at the pictures. They are in the wrong order.
Listen again and number the pictures.

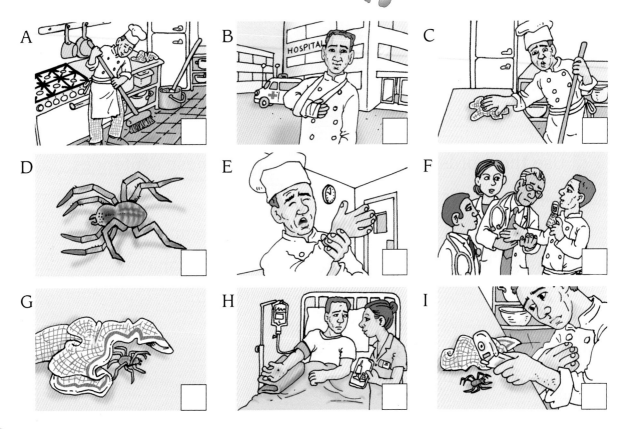

A

B   HOSPITAL

C

D

E

F

G

H

I

4 Can you tell Matthew's story?

Spelling

The letters **ph** in words makes the same sound as **f**.

The tombs of the **pharaohs** had many paintings on the walls.

1 Add *ph* to finish these words. Read the words. Write the words.

1 ele_____ant

_____

2 tele_____one

_____

3 al_____abet

_____

4 dol_____in

_____

5 _____otogra_____

_____

2 Use the words you have made to finish these sentences.

1 I called my friend on the _____.

2 An _____ is a very big animal.

3 You take a _____ with a camera.

4 A _____ lives in the sea.

5 There are 26 letters in the English _____.

3 Tick ✓ the words you can read.

> elephant ☐ telephone ☐ alphabet ☐
> dolphin ☐ photograph ☐

Class writing

Let's write about what people were doing.

Look at these pictures.

What were the people doing when the photographer took the picture? Talk about the pictures then write about them.

The diving lesson

Andy's cousins loved diving. Andy went to stay with them. The next morning his cousins were getting ready to go diving.

'Can you dive, Andy?' Ned asked. Andy shook his head. He was scared of diving but he didn't want to say so.

'Can you swim?' Max asked. Andy nodded. 'Then you can learn to dive,' said Max. 'It's easy.'

When they got to the beach, Ned and Max put all their diving things in the small boat. Max started the motor. It hummed softly. Ned jumped in and Andy watched the boat as it chugged out across the bay.

'Did you want to go with them?' Uncle Roy asked.

'No, thank you, Uncle Roy,' said Andy. 'I'm going to swim.' He ran into the water and swam a little way from the beach. He looked down. There were some fish far below. But the sunlight was shining on the water and he couldn't see them properly.

'I'm going to put my head under the water,' Andy said quietly. 'Then I'm going to see the fish clearly.' Andy took a big breath. He looked down. But he couldn't do it. He was too scared.

When he got back to the beach, Uncle Roy was waiting for him. 'While you were swimming,' he said, 'I was tidying up in the hut. I found this.' He held out a mask with a tube on the side. 'Do you want to try it?' he asked. 'Ned used this when he was learning to dive,' he added.

 Parents: *see extra material on page 166*

Andy said, 'Yes, please.'

Uncle Roy showed him how to put the mask on. He showed him how to breathe through the tube. Together, they swam out from the beach.

'Here's a good place,' said Uncle Roy.

Andy looked down. He could see fish but he couldn't see them properly. 'Now!' he thought. He put his head under the water.

There were hundreds of fish below him, big and small and all different colours. Some fish swam slowly. They flicked their tails gently. Other fish were fast and darted through the seaweed. Andy saw flashes of orange and bright blue. A large pink shell lay on the white sand and red coral covered the rocks.

It all looked very beautiful. Andy spent the morning swimming up and down the bay. He watched sea creatures of every shape and size. He even saw a small manta ray, flapping along the bottom.

When the other boys came back for lunch, Ned saw the mask on Andy's towel. He picked it up. 'This is my old mask,' he said. 'I thought it was lost.'

'I found it in the hut,' said Uncle Roy. 'Andy's using it. He's learning to dive.'

Reading and understanding

1 **Who said this? Write the names.**

1 'Can you dive, Andy?' _____

2 'It's easy.' _____

3 'Did you want to go with them?' _____

4 'I'm going to swim.' _____

5 'Do you want to try it?' _____

6 'Yes, please.' _____

7 'I thought it was lost.' _____

8 'Andy's using it.' _____

2 **Discuss your answers to these questions.**

1 Andy did not want to tell his cousins that he was scared of diving. Why?

2 Does Andy want to learn to dive? How do you know?

3 Why could Andy put his head under the water when he had the mask?

4 Did Uncle Roy find the mask when he was tidying? Did Uncle Roy go and look for the mask? What do you think?

3 **Write the labels.**

| manta ray   coral   shell |
| seaweed   fish |

98 | Comprehension focus | Consolidation of new language in The diving lesson

Working with words

1 **Write the verbs.**

| flap   chug   flick   hum   dart |

sound   _____   _____

movement   _____   _____   _____

2 **Read the phrases. Write the verbs.**

a bird's wings   a bee   a horse's tail   an old car   a mouse

_____   _____   _____   _____   _____

Sentence building

*Remember! A **verb** is a **doing** word. Every sentence has got a verb in it.*

The fish slowly. ☒

This sentence does not make sense.
The **verb** is missing.

The fish swam slowly. ☑

This sentence makes sense.
It has got a **verb** in it.

1 **Choose the correct verb to complete each sentence.**

| read   found   swam   rode   sat   saw |

1 Andy _____ in the sea.

2 Max _____ a book.

3 Ned _____ some fish in the water.

4 Uncle Roy _____ a mask.

5 The old man _____ on the chair.

6 Tom _____ his bike.

Grammar

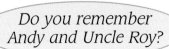

Do you remember Andy and Uncle Roy?

While Uncle Roy **was tidying up** the hut, Andy **was swimming**.

> Remember! These two things were happening at the same time.

1 **Join the pictures. Write the letters.**

1 While the boys were diving, Andy was sitting on the beach. _____ _____

2 While Andy was swimming, Uncle Roy was looking for the mask. _____ _____

3 While little fish were darting through the seaweed, bigger fish were swimming along the bottom. _____ _____

A   B   C   D   E   F

2 **Finish the sentences. Say. Then write.**

1 While Sue was doing her homework, John ...

2 While the boys were playing football, the girls ...

3 While the children were playing, their mother ...

4 While Larry was trying to sleep, his brother ...

Listening

Here's a song about the sea.

1 Talk about the pictures and listen to the song.

Sea Dive

Splash into the waves in a shower of droplets,
Past the _____ skimming o'er the foam.
Leave the _____ screaming, wheeling
Round their cliff-top nesting home.

Down through shoals of darting fishes
Chased by _____ with fearful jaws.
Tuna streaking, _____ squeaking,
_____ cruise by to far-off shores.

Flatfish, _____ move along the sea-bed,
_____ and lobster sideways crawl.
Worms a-wriggling, _____ a-squiggling,
Anemones cling to _____ walls.

Dark and still are the waters of the ocean
Far from the winds and the crashing seas.
Deep down under, gaze with wonder,
Sea green world of mysteries.

Veronica Clark

2 Find these creatures in the pictures. Listen again then write the
missing words. Sing the song!

dolphins	crab	sharks	eels	whales	starfish
	seabirds	coral	flying fish		

Spelling

Compound nouns are made up of two words put together.

sun + light = **sunlight**

1 Choose a word from each box. Label the pictures.

| foot |
| speed |
| home |
| play |
| snow |
| super |

| boat |
| market |
| ball |
| man |
| work |
| ground |

1

snowman

2

_____

3

_____

4

_____

5

_____

6

_____

Spelling focus   *compound nouns*

Class writing

Let's write a story about the sea.

1 Look at the pictures. Read the words.

1

crash   flash   rumble

2

flap   splash   rip

3

sparkle   dart   chug

4

hum   toss   flick

2 Write about the pictures. Use the verbs above.

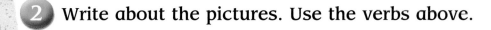

_____

_____

_____

_____

_____

Coral reefs 🎧

Coral reefs look like underwater gardens. The corals look like small plants and bushes. There are corals in every colour of the rainbow. But they are not plants. Corals are many tiny animals growing together. As each animal grows it makes a hard wall all round it. When it dies the hard wall is left and another animal grows on top. Over thousands of years the corals grow bigger and taller. They cover the sea bed for many kilometres. This is called a coral reef.

Corals grow in many different shapes. Some corals look like objects. People named the corals after the objects. There is star coral, rose coral, finger coral and sea fan coral. Some corals do not build reefs. These are the soft corals. There are many of these in the Red Sea. They are beautiful colours and they look like living flowers. Each tiny animal has many arms. These wave in the water and catch even tinier animals for food.

Many wonderful creatures live in a coral reef. Some fish look like animals on land. They have the names of the animals they look like. The parrotfish has a mouth like a parrot's beak. The butterflyfish has spots like a butterfly. The lionfish looks like a lion's head and the clownfish looks like a colourful clown.

Divers must be careful when they swim around the reef. The ray fish with blue spots has a sting in its tail. One little octopus shows blue spots when it is angry. Then it can give a poisonous bite. The red fire coral looks pretty, but it stings.

All the coral reefs are home to ocean wildlife. They are important places in our world but many reefs are in danger. Fishermen and careless divers damage them. Other fish can damage them, too. One strange starfish eats coral. Its name is crown-of-thorns. Usually it swims alone. But fifty years ago thousands of these starfish arrived near Australia and ate many of the corals. Nobody could find out why they did this.

Reading and understanding

1 **Complete the sentences.**

1 Coral reefs look like ＿＿＿＿＿＿＿ gardens.
2 Corals are many tiny ＿＿＿＿＿＿＿ growing together.
3 Some ＿＿＿＿＿＿＿ look like objects.
4 There are many ＿＿＿＿＿＿＿ corals in the Red Sea.
5 Soft corals look like living ＿＿＿＿＿＿＿ .
6 Some ＿＿＿＿＿＿＿ look like animals on land.
7 The ray fish's sting is in its ＿＿＿＿＿＿＿ .
8 The red fire coral can ＿＿＿＿＿＿＿ you.

2 **Discuss the best ending for these sentences. Tick ✓ the box.**

1 Coral reefs look like underwater gardens because

a corals live under water. ☐   b corals are alive. ☐

c corals look like plants. ☐

2 The little octopus with blue spots is dangerous because

a it can get angry. ☐   b it can bite. ☐

c its bite is poisonous. ☐

3 The crown of thorns starfish is strange because

a it has a strange name. ☐   b it looks strange. ☐

c it usually swims alone. ☐

3 **Discuss your answers.**

1 How do you think fishermen damage coral?
2 How do you think divers damage coral?
3 Can you think of other things that damage coral?

Get active 12

Working with words

1 **Which objects and animals do these corals and fish look like? Choose words and match them to the pictures. Write the names.**

| parrot | clown | rose | butterfly | finger | lion |

1 _____

2 _____

3 _____

4 _____

5 _____

6 _____

> Remember! An **adjective** describes a noun. We use a **comparative adjective** when we compare **two** nouns. Many comparative adjectives end with **er**.

Sentence building

This shell is small.

This shell is **smaller**.

This fish is tiny.

This fish is **tinier**.

> Notice the way the spelling changes with this word.

1 **Underline the comparative adjectives.**

1 Ben is <u>noisier</u> than me.　　　　　noisy + er = noisier

2 Ann is pretty but Emma is prettier.　　_____

3 Reading is easier than spelling.　　　_____

4 Max is tidier than Joe.　　　　　　　_____

5 Sam is happy but Amy is happier.　　_____

6 Who is angrier – Ned or Tom?　　　　_____

Grammar

What do you remember about coral reefs?

Fishermen and divers can damage the coral.
Fifty years ago in Australia starfish ate the coral.
Nobody could find out why.

1 **Complete the sentences with *can* or *could*.**

Fifty years ago thousands of starfish arrived near Australia. The starfish ate the coral. People _____ not understand why they did this. Nobody _____ stop them. Now the coral is growing again. You _____ see many wonderful creatures on the coral reef. Most creatures are friendly but some _____ hurt you.

2 **Ask and answer.**

Can you swim?   Yes, I can.   or   No, I can't.

swim   eat   drink   speak

see   hear   run   smile

Think about when you were a baby. Ask and answer again.

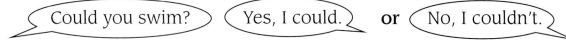

Could you swim?   Yes, I could.   or   No, I couldn't.

3 **Write three things you could do.**
Write three things you could not do.

Remember!
couldn't = could not

Listening

What a great holiday!

The _____ _____ Hotel for the perfect holiday

It's fun for all the family!

1 Listen and write the name of the hotel. 🎧

2 Look at the activities you can do at the hotel. You can ...

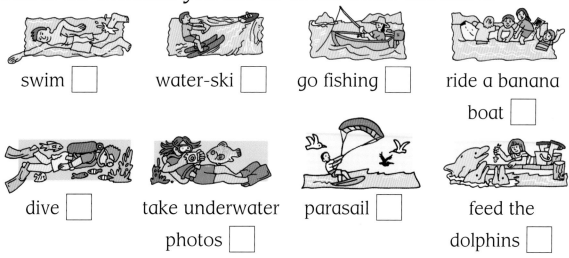

swim ☐   water-ski ☐   go fishing ☐   ride a banana boat ☐

dive ☐   take underwater photos ☐   parasail ☐   feed the dolphins ☐

3 The Scott family went to the hotel for a holiday. Listen and tick ✓ the things they could do. 🎧

4 Listen and say. 🎧

dogfishcatfishlionfishflatfishclownfishjellyfishparrotfishSHARK!

Spelling

When we add **full** to a word, we write it with **one l**.
wonder + full = **wonderful**

Many **wonderful** creatures live in a coral reef.

1 Add *ful* to these words. Read the words. Discuss what each word means. Write the word.

1 play _ful_

playful

2 truth _____

3 use _____

4 cheer _____

5 care _____

6 aw _____

7 pain _____

8 power _____

2 Finish these sentences with some words you have made.

1 Ben is always smiling. He is very _____.

2 Sam never tells lies. He is very _____.

3 The weather is very bad. It is _____.

4 I have hurt my hand. It is very _____.

> If a word ends in **y**, we change the **y** to **i** before we add **ful**.
> beauty + full = **beautiful**

3 Use the word *beautiful* in a sentence of your own.

_____

4 Tick ✓ the words you can read.

> playful ☐   truthful ☐   useful ☐   cheerful ☐   careful ☐
> awful ☐   painful ☐   powerful ☐   beautiful ☐

Class writing

Let's write about life in a coral reef.

What can you see? What colours are there? What do things look like?

Revision 4
You can do it!

1 **Look at the pictures.**
Which picture is the most interesting?
Which picture is the prettiest?
Which one do you like best? Why?
Which one don't you like? Why?

2 **Listen and read.**

3 **Read and say.**
1 Where can people see pictures of coral reefs?
2 What do some crabs live in?
3 When does a crab move to a larger shell?
4 What was the starfish eating?
5 How many arms do starfish have?
6 What do octopuses eat?
7 How many legs does it have?
8 How heavy is a giant clam?

A hundred years ago people could not see all the wonderful fish that live on a coral reef. Now people can see them on TV and in books. Look at all the things that were happening when these pictures were taken.

While the shark was swimming above the rocks, the crab was getting into a shell. When the crab grows bigger it must move to a larger shell.

While the diver was taking a picture of the coral, a starfish was eating it. Some starfish eat other fish. They have five arms and they use them to catch their food.

While the butterflyfish were swimming past the coral, the octopus was catching a crab. An octopus has eight legs and it can see very well.

While the manta ray was swimming along the bottom, the clownfish were swimming behind the giant clam. A clam can weigh up to 180 kg – as much as three people!

4 Listen and find the picture.

5 Read out the descriptions.

6 Write the words.

_____ _____

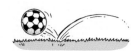

_____ _____

power	cheer
beauty	pain

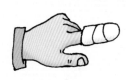

_painful_____ _____

_____ _____

113

Millie's London diary

My diary
Our visit to Grandmother and Grandfather in London, April 1876
by Millie Porter

Monday 21st April
Today Grandmother took John and me to the toyshop. Mr Jolly owns the toy shop. He is very friendly and he is always smiling. He wears a big white apron. He keeps a pencil and a sharp knife in the apron pockets. He can make anything out of wood. He hums while he is working. Grandmother bought some soldiers for John. They are red and blue and they have black hats.

Tuesday 22nd April
This afternoon we went to see Aunt Sara. She lives in a big house near the park. On the way we passed a girl selling flowers. Aunt Sara loves books and I do, too. Today I read some poems to her. I like reading to Aunt Sara. She has a beautiful garden. She showed us her new pond. There wasn't any water in it. The gardener is going to put some water in it tomorrow. Then he is going to put some plants and some fish in it.

Parents: *see extra material on page 166*

Wednesday 23rd April

Grandfather's friend, Mr Brown, came to visit today. He has twinkling eyes. He wears a long black coat and he carries a walking stick. He likes games and puzzles. He brought a puzzle for us. It was a box and some shapes. We had to fit the shapes into the box. He told us funny stories about India. He met an Indian prince once. He gave the prince a puzzle and the prince gave him a monkey!

Thursday 24th April

Today we saw the little flower girl again. She was selling her flowers near the park. She had a large basket full of yellow flowers. She often looks unhappy. She has a thin face. She was wearing an old grey coat but she didn't have any gloves and it was cold today. Grandfather took us for a walk in the park. On the way back he bought some of her flowers. She smiled. She always smiles when someone buys her flowers.

Friday 25th April

A tall policeman often stands at the corner of the street. When we passed him today he said 'Good morning' in a deep, gruff voice. Sometimes he walks past the house. He walks slowly with his hands behind his back and he wears big black boots. He has bushy eyebrows and a big moustache. His eyes are friendly and his cheeks are rosy red. His coat has shiny silver buttons down the front. He looks very smart.

Reading and understanding

1 **Read and circle true (T) or false (F).**

1 Millie's grandmother and grandfather live in London.   T   F
2 Mr Brown owns the toy shop.   T   F
3 Mr Jolly wears an apron.   T   F
4 Millie read a story to Aunt Sara.   T   F
5 An Indian prince gave Mr Brown a puzzle.   T   F
6 The flower girl was selling her flowers in the park.   T   F
7 Grandfather bought some of her flowers.   T   F
8 The policeman said 'Goodbye' in a deep, gruff voice.   T   F

2 **Discuss your answers to these questions.**

1 Why does Mr Jolly have a pencil and a sharp knife in his apron pocket?
2 Does Millie like Aunt Sara? How do you know?
3 Is Mr Brown a happy person? How do you know?
4 Can you think why the flower girl is often unhappy?
5 Do you think the policeman likes his job? How do you know?

3 **Who do these things belong to?**

   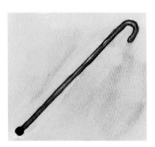

Get active 13

Working with words

1 Millie used these adjectives to describe things. Match them with the nouns below. Write the phrases.

| 1 ~~twinkling~~ | 2 rosy | 3 shiny | 4 gruff | 5 bushy | 6 thin |

| eyebrows | face | voice | ~~eyes~~ | cheeks | buttons |

1 _twinkling eyes_   2 _____

3 _____   4 _____

5 _____   6 _____

Sentence building

*Remember! A **pronoun** takes the place of a **noun**. A **personal pronoun** takes the place of a **person** or **thing**.*

The policeman is tall. **He** is very smart.

This is a **personal pronoun**.
He means 'the policeman'.

Here are some personal pronouns:

| I | me | you | he | him | she | her | it | we | us | they | them |

1 Find the personal pronouns. What nouns do they replace?

1 The girl is thin. <u>She</u> looks unhappy. ___the girl_____

2 The children are running. They are playing a game. _____

3 The dog is barking. It is hungry. _____

4 Tom likes Sarah but he does not like Anna. _____

5 Mrs Hill asked Ben, 'Do you want a sweet?' _____

Grammar

Do you remember Millie Porter's diary?

Is there any water in it?
There isn't any water in it.
The gardener is going to put some water in it.

Has she got any gloves?
She hasn't got any gloves.
There are some yellow flowers in her basket.

---

1 Ask and answer.

Is there any water in the glass?

Yes, there is. **or** No, there isn't.

1 2  3  4

water – bottle   bread – plate   fruit – bowl   juice – glass

Are there any flowers in the basket?

Yes, there are. **or** No, there aren't.

5  6  7  8

toys – shop   fish – pond   buttons – coat   soldiers – box

2 Say. Then write.

1 There isn't any water in the bottle.
2 There is some bread on the plate.
3 _____
4 _____
5 There are some toys in the shop.
6 There aren't any fish in the pond.
7 _____
8 _____

Grammar focus   some *and* any

Listening

Listen to Millie.

13

1 Look at the pictures below. Describe them.

2 Listen to Millie.
How many mistakes did she make? Write the numbers.

3 Listen again. Correct Millie's mistakes.

4 Listen and sing.

Come and buy my roses! Sweet, sweet roses!
Come and buy my roses!
Come and buy!

Lovely roses! Pretty posies!
Lovely roses! Pretty posies!

Come and buy my roses! Sweet, sweet roses!
Come and buy my roses!
Come and buy!

Listening focus   *listening for detail*

Spelling

When we add **un** to the beginning of words, we can make **opposites**.

The little flower girl often looks **unhappy**.
happy   **unhappy**

1 **Put *un* in front of these words. Make opposites.**

1 do   _____do   2 cover   _____cover

3 pack   _____pack   4 fair   _____fair

5 well   _____well   6 wrap   _____wrap

7 true   _____true   8 kind   _____kind

2 **Solve the clues with some of the *un* words you have made.**

1 take the paper off a present   _ _ _ _ _ _

2 take things out of a suitcase   _ _ _ _ _ _

3 feeling ill   _ _ _ _ _ _

4 A lie is this.   _ _ _ _ _ _

5 not nice to someone   _ _ _ _ _ _

3 **Tick ✓ the correct answer.**

1 Someone who is untidy is   very tidy. ☐   not tidy. ☐

2 Someone who is unhappy is   very happy. ☐   not happy. ☐

3 Someone who is unfair is   very fair. ☐   not fair. ☐

4 **Tick ✓ the words you can read.**

undo ☐   uncover ☐   unpack ☐   unfair ☐   unwell ☐
unwrap ☐   untrue ☐   unkind ☐   untidy ☐   unhappy ☐

Class writing

Let's describe somebody.

1 **This is Aunt Sara's gardener, Mr Green. Look carefully at the picture.**

Think about these questions:

1 What clothes is he wearing?
2 What colour are they?
3 How does he look?
4 What does he use?

2 **Describe Aunt Sara's gardener.**

The Romans

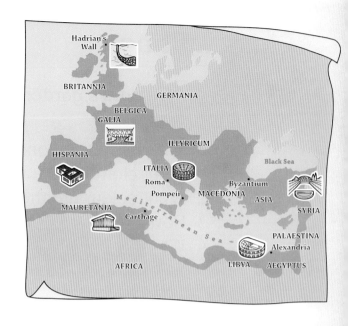

A long time ago the Roman people made Rome into a big, strong city. The Romans were good soldiers. They travelled a long way from Rome. They built roads, cities and bridges in all the countries that they went to. Everyone in those countries had to obey the Romans. They had to pay a lot of money to them. The Romans called all these countries the Roman Empire.

The Roman roads were straight. It is quicker to walk along a straight road. Sometimes people disobeyed the Romans. The soldiers marched along the roads and arrived quickly. They made the people obey them. The soldiers helped to build the roads.

First they marked a straight line.

Then they dug down 1 metre.

After that they put down big stones.

Next they covered the big stones with small stones.

Sometimes they put flat stones on top.

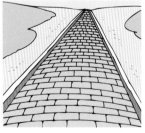

The top of the road was curved.

Rainwater ran off into the ditches.

The army could march in bad weather. There was not much water on the road and the carts did not get stuck in mud. Everybody could use the roads.

metal helmet

spear

metal armour

woollen tunic

knife

metal belt

sword

thick sandals

Every Roman soldier had good clothes. He had a metal helmet. It protected his head. Metal armour protected his body. He had a woollen tunic. It kept him warm. The soldier's belt was metal. He kept his knife on the belt. He had a sword and he had a spear. He had sandals on his feet. They were thick because soldiers had to march on hard roads.

A good soldier became a leader. He led a hundred men. He had a red cloak and red feathers on his helmet. Red was the colour for Roman soldiers.

Soldiers learned to drive chariots. Two, three or four horses pulled the chariot. It could carry one or two people. It was not heavy and it could go fast. The driver was the charioteer. He used a whip to make the horses go faster. The other soldier was often a bowman and he used a bow and arrow. In Rome many people liked to watch chariot races. These races were exciting but they were dangerous. Sometimes the chariots crashed.

Reading and understanding

1 **Answer these questions.**

1 What city did the Romans come from?

_____

2 What did the Romans build in other countries?

_____

3 Who helped to build the roads?

_____

4 What metal objects did a Roman soldier wear?

_____

5 What did the metal helmet do?

_____

6 What colour clothes did Roman soldiers wear?

_____

7 What did soldiers learn to drive?

_____

2 **Find the answers to these questions.**

1 What did people in the Roman empire have to do?
2 Why did the Romans build straight roads?
3 There was not much water on the roads in bad weather.
Why not?

3 **Discuss answers to these questions.**

1 Why do you think people sometimes disobeyed the Romans?
2 Why do you think the Romans used metal for helmets and armour?
3 Were Roman soldiers important people? Why?

Get active 14

Working with words

1 Write the opposite meaning.

1 straight _____ 2 obey _____ 3 safe _____

4 thin _____ 5 weak _____ 6 slower _____

7 nobody _____ 8 boring _____

2 Use the correct word to complete these sentences.

1 People did not always do what the Romans told them and they

_____ them.

2 Chariot races were interesting and they were never_____ .

Sentence building

> **Rule 1:** If a verb ends with a **vowel + y,** we add **ed** in the past tense.
>
>
>
> The children **played** a game.
> play + ed = played

> **Rule 2:** If a verb ends with a **consonant + y,** we change the **y** to **i** and add **ed** in the past tense.
>
> The soldier **carried** a sword.
> carry + ed = carried

1 Write the past tense of each verb. Discuss which rule you use.

verb	past tense	rule
cry	cried	2
try	_____	___
stay	_____	___
enjoy	_____	___
hurry	_____	___
obey	_____	___

2 Make up some sentences. Use the past tense of the verbs in them.

Grammar

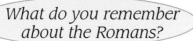

What do you remember about the Romans?

> **How many** people liked to watch chariot races?
> **Lots of** people.   OR   **A lot of** people.
> **How much** time did they spend at the stadium?
> **Lots of** time.   OR   **A lot of** time.

1 **Ask and answer.**

soldiers
How many soldiers are there?   Lots of soldiers.

money
How much money is there?   Lots of money.

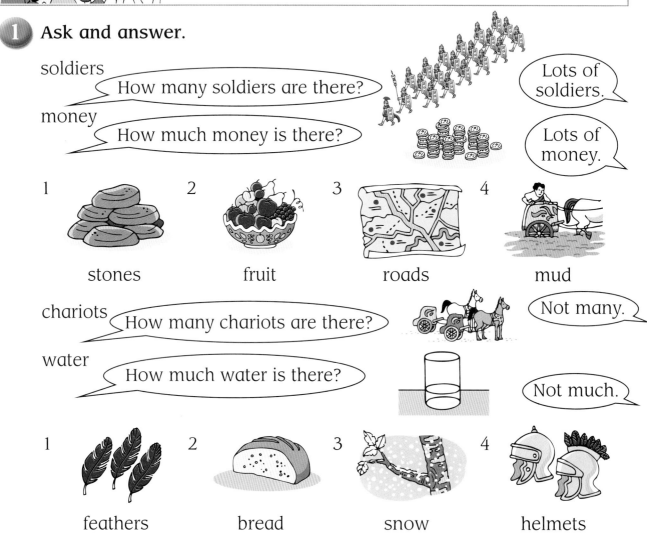

1 stones   2 fruit   3 roads   4 mud

chariots
How many chariots are there?   Not many.

water
How much water is there?   Not much.

1 feathers   2 bread   3 snow   4 helmets

2 **Say. Then write.**

people – food   There are lots of people but there isn't much food.
rivers – bridges   There are lots of rivers but there aren't many bridges.

1 children – books   2 fruit – vegetables
3 bread – butter   4 biscuits – juice

Grammar focus   *countable and uncountable nouns with* How many...? *and* How much...?

Listening

Listen to an exciting chariot race.

Four charioteers were in a race.

Marcus   Aquila   Cassius   Brutus

1 **Listen. Write the correct names under the chariots.**

_____   _____

_____   _____

2 **Listen. Who won the race?**

3 **Listen and sing.**

Rumpety, tumpety, tumpety, tump.
  Here comes the galloping major!
Rumpety, tumpety, tumpety, tump.
  Here comes the galloping major!
All the people cry as he goes galloping by,
"Hey! Hey! Get out of the way!
  Here comes the galloping major!"

Spelling

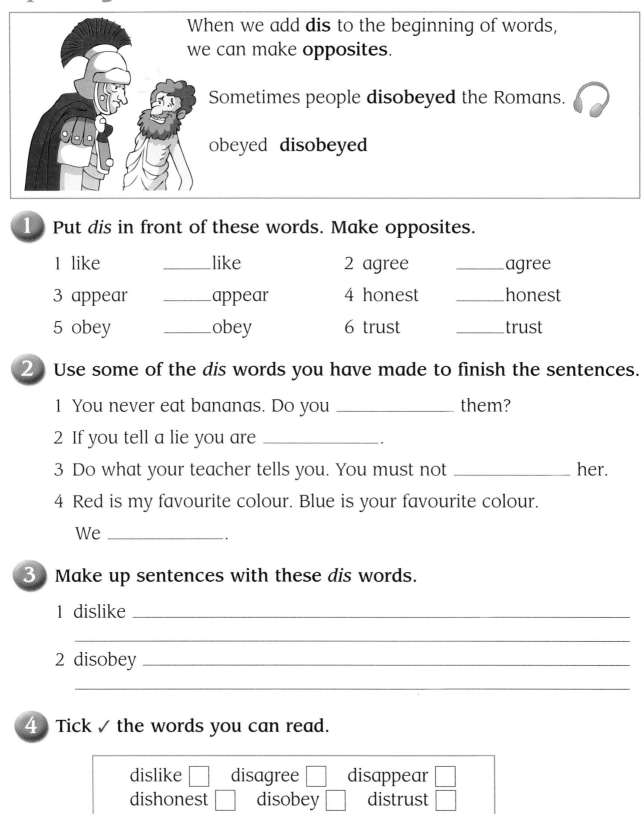

When we add **dis** to the beginning of words, we can make **opposites**.

Sometimes people **disobeyed** the Romans.

obeyed **disobeyed**

1 **Put *dis* in front of these words. Make opposites.**

1 like _____like

2 agree _____agree

3 appear _____appear

4 honest _____honest

5 obey _____obey

6 trust _____trust

2 **Use some of the *dis* words you have made to finish the sentences.**

1 You never eat bananas. Do you _____ them?

2 If you tell a lie you are _____.

3 Do what your teacher tells you. You must not _____ her.

4 Red is my favourite colour. Blue is your favourite colour.

We _____.

3 **Make up sentences with these *dis* words.**

1 dislike _____

_____

2 disobey _____

_____

4 **Tick ✓ the words you can read.**

dislike ☐ disagree ☐ disappear ☐
dishonest ☐ disobey ☐ distrust ☐

Class writing

Let's write about Roman Chariots.

1 Label the picture. Write a short description of the chariot and the people in it.

> chariot   wheel   whip   horse   charioteer
> bowman   bow   arrow

2 Label the picture. Write a short description of the Roman centurion.

> helmet   armour   tunic   belt   knife
> feathers   sword   sandals   cloak

Delicious ice cream

Ice cream dream

Ice cream, oh, ice cream,
I dream of ice cream!

Ice cream is soft.
Ice cream is creamy.
Ice cream is wonderful.
Ice cream is dreamy.

Ice cream, oh, ice cream,
I dream of ice cream!

Ice cream with strawberries,
Ice cream with pears,
I like eating ice cream
sitting on the stairs.

Ice cream, oh, ice cream,
I dream of ice cream!

Ice cream in a glass,
Ice cream in a cone,
I can eat an ice cream
and talk on the phone.

Ice cream, oh, ice cream,
I dream of ice cream!

Ice cream is frozen.
Ice cream is cold.
I'll eat ice cream
even when I'm old.

Ice cream, oh, ice cream,
I dream of ice cream!

I eat ice cream.
I can't stop.
I'll eat ice cream
until I POP!

Ice cream, oh, ice cream,
I dream of ice cream!

   Parents: *see extra material on page 166*

Space lolly

A Roaring Rocket
is the lolly from Mars!
I know because the wrapper
has planets and stars.

Come on, quick, Mum!
Push the trolley,
through the check-out,
Thanks for my lolly!

Tear off the paper,
drop it in the bin.
My green ice-rocket!
I can't wait to begin.

Bite off the top
so cold and sweet,
cools me down
from my head to my feet.

A taste of lemon,
it's going so fast.
The trouble with lollies is
they don't last.

Just half a mouthful,
a final lick.
All gone now, there's
nothing but the stick.

Choose, please!

Pineapple, chocolate
coffee or cherry?
Orange or lemon,
mint or strawberry?
Coconut, melon,
banana or lime?
Please, tell me the flavour
you want this time!

Reading and understanding

1 **Write the words.**

Poem 1: Ice cream dream

   1 Find four adjectives to describe ice cream. ____ ____ ____ ____

   2 Find the place where the poet likes to eat ice cream. _____

   3 Find two things to put ice cream in. _____ _____

   4 Find the word that means 'very cold'. _____

   5 Find a word for a loud sound. _____

Poem 2: Space lolly

   6 Find the object the ice lolly looks like. _____

   7 Find two things that are on the wrapper. _____ _____

   8 Find the fruit in the poem. _____

   9 Find the thing that is left at the end. _____

Poem 3: Choose, please!

  10 How many flavours are in the poem? _____

2 **Discuss your answers to these questions.**

   1 Where did the boy's mother buy the lolly? Which words tell you?
   2 Which fruits does the girl like with ice cream? Which other fruits do
      you think go well with ice cream? Make a list.
   3 Look at the last poem. What flavour ice cream do you like best?
      Do you know any other flavours of ice cream?
   4 Is it good to eat a lot of ice cream? Why? or Why not?

3 **Which of these fruits are not mentioned in any of the poems?**

Get active 15

Working with words

1 **Find the rhyming pairs.**

| quick   pocket   sweet   stare   phone   eat   own   chair   lick   rocket |

_____   _____   _____   _____   _____

_____   _____   _____   _____   _____

Sentence building

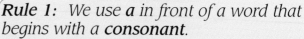

Rule 1: *We use **a** in front of a word that begins with a **consonant**.*
Rule 2: *We use **an** in front of a word that begins with a vowel (**a**, **e**, **i**, **o** or **u**).*

a red lolly   **an** orange lolly

1 **Choose *a* or *an* for each gap. Which rule did you use?**

a big ball
(rule 1)

__ empty glass
(rule __)

__ ice cream
(rule __)

__ tall giant
(rule __)

__ unhappy child
(rule __)

__ heavy box
(rule __)

__ old man
(rule __)

__ cold drink
(rule __)

__ yellow banana
(rule __)

Grammar

Do you like ice cream?

Would you like **a** lolly?
Would you like **an** enormous lolly?
The lolly in your hand is melting!

Lollies are nice in summer.
The lollies in this shop are great.

I love ice cream.
The ice cream in this cafe is delicious.

1 Ask and answer.

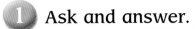

What is it?

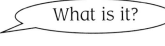

It's a lolly.

What are they?

They're lollies.

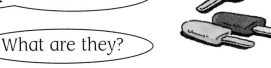

1   2  3   4   5   6

2 What has she got? Say.

1    2    3

4

She has got grapes and a pineapple. The grapes are green and the pineapple is orange.

3 Write *the* or nothing at all in the gaps.

1 I like _____ coffee but _____ coffee in the pot is cold.
2 Our baker sells _____ fresh bread. I like _____ bread from his shop.
3 We love _____ ice cream in this cafe. We buy _____ ice cream every weekend.

Listening

Mmm! Delicious!

An ice cream surprise!
You need:

| cake | fruit | ice cream | a cherry or a strawberry |

1 **Cover the pictures below and listen.**

What does the ice cream surprise look like?

A

B

2 **Look at the pictures. Listen again.**

Number the pictures in the correct order.

A   B   C

D   E   F

G   H   I

3 **Listen and say.**

Ice cream, nice cream, ice cream, nice cream, ice cream, nice cream, ice cream, NICE!

Spelling

The letter **c** in some words makes a sound like **s**.
It is called **soft c**.

I like **ice** cream.

The letter **c** makes a sound
like **s** when it is followed by:

the letter **e**   the letter **i**   the letter **y**

mice   circle   bicycle

1 Add a *soft c* to these words. Read the words. Write the words.

1

pen__il

_____

2

fa__e

_____

3

__ircle

_____

4

prin__e

_____

5

sli__e

_____

6

jui__e

_____

2 Use some of the *soft c* words to solve these clues.

1 You can draw with this.   __ __ __ __ __ __

2 You can drink this.   __ __ __ __ __

3 You cut a piece of bread or cake into this.   __ __ __ __ __

4 This is round.   __ __ __ __ __ __

3 Tick ✓ the words you can read.

pencil ☐   circle ☐   prince ☐   slice ☐   juice ☐

ice cream ☐   rice ☐   mice ☐

Class writing

Let's finish a poem.

1 **Look at the pictures. Read the poem. Write the best words to complete the verses.**

_____

White ice,

_____ leap,   whales   seals

_____ seals   grey   funny

dive _____.   down   deep

White ice,

_____ air,   freezing   windy

_____ snow,   clean   sparkling

polar _____.   star   bear

White ice,

_____ sky.   blue   tall

_____ fox   little   quickly

running _____.   past   by

2 **Read your poem. Think of a title.
Write it on the line at the top.**

Revision 5
You can do it!

1 **Look at the pictures.**
Do you like biscuits?
Do you like cakes?
What cake do you like best?
What do you like to drink?

2 **Listen and read.**

3 **Read and say.**
1 Who wants some orange juice?
2 Who wants some tea?
3 Who doesn't want any tea?
4 Are there many cherry cakes?
5 Is there much chocolate ice cream?
6 Who likes strawberry ice cream?
7 Is there much sugar?
8 Are there many biscuits?
9 Is there much milk in the jug?

Grandfather, grandmother, Sarah and Paul are going to have tea in the tea shop.

4 Listen and look at the last picture. Name the person.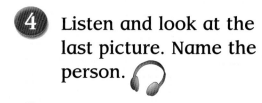

5 Act the story.

6 Write the words.

un …

_____   _____

dis …

_____   _____

_____   _____

Glass

People made glass 4,000 years ago. They heated sand in a fire. When sand gets very hot it melts. It makes a thick, sticky liquid. While the liquid is cooling, it is easy to shape it. The first glass makers shaped round beads. These were the first glass objects.

Later, Egyptian people made vases from glass. They used earth to make the shape. They heated the sand. They dripped the hot liquid onto the shape. They completely covered the shape then they let the liquid cool. When it was hard they picked out the earth from the middle. It took a long time to make a vase in this way.

Next, people learned to blow glass. This was quicker and cheaper so more people could have glass things. The Romans often had glass bottles and jars in their homes.

People still blow glass. This glass blower has a long, thin metal pipe. First he picks up some of the thick liquid. He blows into the pipe. The shape at the other end gets bigger. He uses a piece of wood to shape it and when it is the right shape he cuts it off the pipe.

People learned to make different shapes. This light has shapes like raindrops. There are hundreds of pieces of glass in it. The candles shine on the glass. The glass makes the light shine more brightly.

A painter sometimes paints glass with gold and bright colours. You can decorate an empty glass jar with coloured paper and make it into a present. But, remember! You must always ask an adult before you make something like this.

How to make a sweet jar

You need
a clean, empty glass jar
A4 white paper
crayons or coloured pens

scissors
glue
40 cms of ribbon, string or wool
some sweets (or nuts)

1 Measure 20 cms along the paper. Draw a line. Cut the paper.

2 Cut the small piece of paper into 3 pieces.

3 Choose 3 colours. Colour the pieces.

4 Cut out shapes.

5 Stick the shapes on the jar.

6 Draw a circle on the big piece of paper.

7 Cut it out. Draw and colour a pattern.

8 Put the sweets in the jar.

9 Put the paper circle on top of the jar.

10 Tie the ribbon round the jar.

Give it as a present.

Reading and understanding

1 **Read and circle true (T) or false (F).**

1	People melted sand to make the first glass.	T	F
2	The first glass objects were vases.	T	F
3	Egyptian people used sand to make a shape.	T	F
4	The Romans had glass bottles and vases in their homes.	T	F
5	A glass blower blows into a bottle.	T	F
6	He uses a metal pipe to shape the glass.	T	F
7	There are only a few pieces of glass in the light.	T	F

2 **Complete the sentences.**

1 You need _____ to cut the paper.

2 You need _____ to colour the paper.

3 You need _____ to stick the paper.

4 You need a piece of ribbon _____ cms long.

5 You draw a line _____ cms from one end of the paper.

6 You can put sweets or _____ in the jar.

3 **Discuss your answers to these questions.**

1 Why did the Egyptian vases take a long time to make?
2 Do you think the light took a long time to make? Why?
3 Why must you ask an adult before you make something?

Get active 16

Working with words

 Write the words. All these objects are made of glass.

1 You look in this to see your face.
2 This usually has liquid in it.
3 These were the first glass objects.
4 You look through this.
5 You can pour water out of this.
6 This usually has food in it.
7 You can drink out of this.

Sentence building

*A conjunction can **join** two sentences together.*

Don't go near the fire. It is hot.
Don't go near the fire **because** it is hot.

I put beads on a string. I can make a necklace.
I put beads on a string **so** I can make a necklace.

 Underline the conjunctions. Discuss which two sentences each conjunction joins.

1 I am eating a sandwich <u>because</u> I am hungry.
2 The girl opens the door so she can go into her house.
3 The boy is smiling because he is happy.
4 The girl is picking flowers so she can give them to her mum.
5 I am going to bed because I am tired.
6 I am holding a pen so I can write a letter.

Grammar

What do you remember about glass?

The Romans often had glass jars in their homes.
Roman glass was usually very beautiful.
Painters sometimes paint glass with bright colours.
You must always be careful with glass objects.
You must never drop a glass bottle.

1 **Put the words in the correct place in the sentences.**

1 usually – Glass making is a difficult job.

2 sometimes – Glassmakers blow glass.

3 always – You must hold glass carefully.

4 never – You must throw stones at glass.

5 often – Old glass is very beautiful.

> Remember! These words go …
> **after** the verb *to be*
> **before** all other verbs
> **between** two verbs.

2 **Write sentences.**

Look at this:

never ⟶ sometimes ⟶ often ⟶ usually ⟶ always

1 go to bed late   *I sometimes go to bed late.*

2 get up early   _____

3 late for school   _____

4 do my homework   _____

3 **Ask and answer with a friend.**

I sometimes go to bed late. How about you?

I sometimes go to bed late, too.

I never go to bed late.

Listening

Listen to Professor Inkspot.

1 Can you name these objects? They are either made of glass or have glass parts.

A   B   C   D

E   F   G   H

I   J   K   L

M   N   O   P

Find the words in the word snakes.

vasefishbowlclockmicroscopebottlelightglassmirror

telescopewindowglassesjarnecklacejugbinocularsclock

2 Do you remember Professor Inkspot?
Listen to him talking about glass.

1 Is he talking about glass
   a at home?   b at school?   c in the street?

2 Does he think that glass is useful or not?

3 Listen again.
Which objects in Exercise 1 does he talk about?

4 Listen and say.

Two fat drops of rain
Running down the window pane,
Moving at a steady pace.
Which one's going to win the race?

Larry Left or Ricky Right?
Moving faster … What a fight!
It's Ricky Right! Hooray! He's won!
And look! Here comes the sun!

Spelling

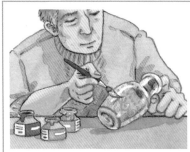 We can add the letters **er** to some verbs to make nouns.

He **paints** glass with gold and bright colours.

He is a **painter**.

verb = paint   noun = **painter**

1 Add *er* to these verbs to make nouns. Read the words. Write the words.

1 sing_____

2 build_____

3 teach_____

_____   _____   _____

If the word ends in a **short vowel** + **a consonant**, double the consonant before adding **er**.

swim + m + er = swimmer

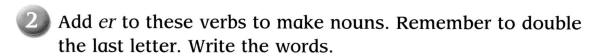

2 Add *er* to these verbs to make nouns. Remember to double the last letter. Write the words.

1 shop_____

2 run_____

3 win_____

_____   _____   _____

3 Tick ✓ the words you can read.

singer ☐	teacher ☐	shopper ☐	winner ☐
builder ☐	painter ☐	runner ☐	swimmer ☐

Class writing

Let's write how to make a necklace.

How to make a necklace

You need:

_____   _____   _____   _____

1 _____   2 _____

3 _____   4 _____

5 _____   6 _____

7 _____

Eddie, the Emerald Island Detective

Parents: see extra material on page 166

Reading and understanding

1 Answer the questions.

1 What is Eddie's job?

_____

2 Where does Professor Trench work?

_____

3 When did Professor Trench dig up the vase?

_____

4 Where did the policemen look for the thieves?

_____

5 How did Eddie and the Inspector get to the big ship quickly?

_____

6 How did Professor Trench get to the big ship?

_____

7 Where did Eddie see a picture of Smokey?

_____

2 Discuss answers to these questions.

1 Why was the vase called the Emerald Vase?
2 Why did the policemen look in people's suitcases?
3 What was in the black bag on the small boat?
4 Why did the men in the small boat have a rope?
5 What was the orange ball for?
6 How did Smokey help Eddie?
7 Who do you think helped to find the vase, Smokey or Eddie?

Get active 17

Comprehension focus   Consolidation of new language in Eddie, the Detective

Working with words

 Match the words in the box with a word below that has a similar meaning. Write the words.

inspector	bag	~~boat~~	realise	sailors	clever	thief

1 ship   __boat__   2 robber   _____

3 suitcase   _____   4 policeman   _____

5 understand   _____   6 crew   _____

7 intelligent   _____

Sentence building

You are the **cleverest** cat in the world.

*Remember! An **adjective** describes a **noun**.*

clever (adjective)   clever**est** (superlative adjective)

We use a **superlative adjective** to compare **more than two** nouns.
We often add **est** to an adjective to make it into a superlative.

 Underline the superlative adjective in each sentence. Write the adjective and the superlative adjective.

	adjective	superlative
1 Tom is the <u>tallest</u> child in our class.	tall	tallest
2 The book is the oldest book in the library.	_____	_____
3 The boy chose the cake that tasted the sweetest.	_____	_____
4 What is the shortest day of the year?	_____	_____
5 The Nile is the longest river in Africa.	_____	_____
6 An ant is the smallest insect I know.	_____	_____

Grammar

Do you remember
Eddie and Smokey?

'Can we help
you, Professor?'

'Can I look in your
suitcase, please?'

 1 Match the questions and the answers.

1 Can we help you, Professor?
2 Can I see your passport, please?
3 Can I borrow your binoculars?
4 Can I ask you some questions, please?
5 Can I take a photo of the cat?

a Yes, of course. Here they are.
b Certainly. What do you want to know?
c Of course. Here he is.
d I'm sorry. I don't know where it is.
e Oh, yes please, Eddie.

2 Read. Then ask.

Your friend is going to spend the day at your house.
There is a good programme on TV.
You would like to have sandwiches for lunch.
It is a hot day and there is a swimming pool near your house.
You have some new computer games.
You would like your friend to stay the night.
You would like to go to bed late.

Before you do these things, you must ask your parents. What questions do you ask?

Please, can we …?   Can we …, please?

Listening

Here's a tricky puzzle for you!

Who stole Mrs Honeypot's necklace? Was it ... ?

Where's my necklace?

Stan Brown

Brian West

Nadia Bows

Wes Stoner

1 Look at the map and listen carefully.
Find the letters and write them in your notebook.

2 Look at the letters in your notebook. Can you find the name of the thief? Write it here: _____

3 Listen and sing.

Watch out, watch out! There's a thief about.
Shut your windows! Lock your doors!
Gold and silver shining brightly,
Sparkling diamonds he likes best.

Quick as a flash he picks them up
And flies away to his nest.

Spelling

We can break words into small parts. These are called **syllables**.
Each syllable has a **vowel sound**.

one syllable word
vase ⬤

two syllable word
island ⬤

1 Say the words. Discuss how many syllables there are.

1
boat

2
diver

3
dolphin

4
pencil

5
face

6
paint

2 Write the words under the correct heading.

one syllable words

_____

_____

_____

two syllable words

_____

_____

_____

The letter **y** can sometimes stand in place of a **vowel**.

baby

teddy

3 Say the words. Discuss how many syllables there are.

1 puppy   2 sky   3 lorry   4 fly   5 lady   6 boy

4 Tick ✓ the words you can read.

boat ☐   diver ☐   face ☐   dolphin ☐   paint ☐   pencil ☐
sky ☐   puppy ☐   fly ☐   lorry ☐   boy ☐   lady ☐

Class writing

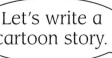
Let's write a cartoon story.

Professor Trench is showing Eddie a box. Eddie thinks it is a very strange box.

Professor Trench cannot open the box. Eddie can help him.

Professor Trench shows Eddie the pictures. Eddie thinks the pictures are a message.

Professor Trench says all the pictures are fish. Eddie says he must look closely.

Smokey puts his paw on the fish. Eddie tells Smokey to be careful.

Suddenly the box opens. Eddie says Smokey is clever. Professor Trench looks in the box.

The selfish giant

Every day after school some children played in a beautiful garden. It belonged to a giant but he was not in his castle. He was visiting his friend a long way away. Flowers like stars grew in the grass. In spring the trees had pink flowers on their branches. In the autumn the trees held round golden fruit.

'We are very happy here!' the children told each other.

The giant stayed away for seven years, but one day he came back. He saw the children in his garden. 'What are you doing here?' he asked in a gruff voice. 'This garden is mine!' The children ran away. The giant built a wall all round the garden. He put up a big notice: KEEP OUT!

He was a very selfish giant. The children had nowhere to play. They tried to play on the road, but the road was very dusty and full of hard stones. They passed the high wall after school. 'We were happy there,' they said to each other.

Spring came. Everywhere there were flowers and birds. But in the selfish giant's garden it was still winter. The birds did not want to sing in it because there were no children. There were no flowers anywhere. Snow covered the grass. The north wind came. It rattled the windows. It roared all round the garden like an angry beast. The giant could not understand it. 'Where is spring?' he said.

But spring never came, nor the summer. In the autumn the other gardens had golden fruit but the giant's garden had nothing. It was always winter in his garden. There was ice and snow. The cold north wind blew more fiercely every day.

One morning the giant woke up early. He heard beautiful music. It was a bird singing cheerfully outside his window. The giant looked out. He saw a small hole in his tall, thick wall. But then he saw the most wonderful sight. In every tree sat a little child. Pink flowers were on the branches. The birds were flying about and twittering. The flowers nodded their heads most joyfully. The giant's heart melted.

'I was very selfish!' he said. 'Now I understand why spring never came! My garden can be the children's playground for ever and ever!' He took a big axe and knocked down the wall and the children played there every day.

Reading and understanding

1 **Choose the correct ending.**

1 The children played in the garden _____ .
   a in the spring   b after school   c after lunch

2 In spring, the branches on the trees had pink _____ .
   a fruit   b sweets   c flowers

3 The trees held golden fruit _____ .
   a in the autumn   b in the garden   c for the children

4 The giant stayed away for seven _____ .
   a days   b years   c weeks

5 The giant built a wall around _____ .
   a the children   b the castle   c the garden

6 The notice said: _____ !
   a Keep away   b Keep out   c Look out

7 In the giant's garden it was always _____ .
   a ice   b wind   c cold

8 When the giant woke up he heard beautiful _____ .
   a music   b children   c a bird

9 In the garden he saw _____ .
   a a child   b children   c a hole

10 He took an axe and knocked down _____ .
   a the castle   b the trees   c the wall

2 **Discuss answers for these questions.**

1 Why were the children happy in the garden at first?
2 Why did the children run away when the giant came back?
3 How did the children get into the garden again?
4 Why did spring come back to the giant's garden?
5 Why did he knock the wall down?
6 Was the giant sorry for being selfish? How do you know?

Get active 18

Working with words

1 **Find and write the correct word.**

| joyfully   rattle   twitter   fiercely   cheerfully   roar |

1 The sound the windows made when the wind blew hard against them. _____

2 The sound the wind made when it blew around the garden.
_____

3 Two words that mean 'happily'. _____ / _____

4 One word that means 'angrily and unkindly'. _____

5 The sound birds make when they are happy. _____

Sentence building

This is my garden.

We can write what the giant said in **two ways**.
'This is my garden,' the giant said.
The giant said, 'This is my garden.'

Remember! We write what a person says inside **speech marks**.

1 **Write each sentence in another way.**

1 'We like the garden,' the children said.

_____

2 The giant said, 'I am selfish.'

_____

2 **Write this in two different ways.**

I am very sad.

1 _____

2 _____

Grammar

Do you remember the selfish giant?

> Winter came and the cold wind blew fiercely.
> It blew more fiercely every day.
> It blew the most fiercely in the giant's garden.

1 Change the sentences.

1 The birds sang a sweet song. The birds sang ___sweetly___.

2 The children sang a cheerful song. The children sang _____.

3 The children had happy smiles. The children smiled _____.

2 Ask and answer.

animal – run – quickly

Which animal can run more quickly?

The horse can run more quickly.

1

animal – growl – fiercely

2

person – pull – strongly

3

person – sing – sweetly

4

animal – walk – quietly

3 Make sentences.

A   B   C

2 A   B   C

run – quickly

3 A   B   C

shine – brightly

1 ___C sings the most loudly.___

Listening

 Who likes who?

 Listen to the children. Who are friends?

Sue

Paddy

Daisy

Tom

Lisa

Friends are special when they sing together,
They can sing the whole day,
They can sing the night away,
They can sing together, they can sing.

Friends are special when they laugh together,
They can laugh the whole day,
They can laugh the night away,
They can laugh together, they can laugh.

Friends are special when they cry together,
They can cry the whole day,
They can cry the night away,
They can cry together, they can cry.

Friends are special when they dream together,
They can dream the whole day,
They can dream the night away,
They can dream together, they can dream.

Maisie

Paul

Carol

Henry

Jodi

 Listen and sing.

Spelling

The letters **ch** can make a **soft** sound.

The **children** played in the beautiful garden.

The letters **ch** can make a **hard** sound like **k**.

They played after **school**.

1 Which words have a *soft ch*? Which words have a *hard ch*?

1 chair

2  choir

3  lunch

4 chicken

5 anchor

6 stomach

2 Write the words under the correct heading.

soft *ch* words

_____

_____

_____

hard *ch* words

_____

_____

_____

3 Complete these words with *soft ch*. Read the words.

1 ____ild   2 ____eese   3 ____eck

4 ri____   5 tor ____   6 mar____

4 Tick ✓ the words you can read.

chair ☐   check ☐   lunch ☐   anchor ☐   chicken ☐   rich ☐
stomach ☐   child ☐   torch ☐   choir ☐   cheese ☐   march ☐

Class writing

Let's write a story.

1 **Look at the pictures. Think about the story.**
What can you see in the giant's garden? What happened in his garden?
Think about the verbs you know. How do birds fly in the sky? How do
they sound? Think about adjectives for colours and sizes of things.
Think about adverbs. How are the children playing?

2 **Think of a strong opening for the story. Write the story.**

Writing focus   *a descriptive story*

Revision 6
You can do it!

1 **Look at the picture.**
Do you like gardens?
Why or why not?
What do you like in
this garden?

2 **Listen and read.**

3 **Read and say.**
1 Find the girl with
long black hair. What
does she often do?
2 What does the girl
with the pink dress
want to do?
3 What are always in
the orange flowers?
4 Where are the shells?
5 Which flowers grow
most quickly?
6 Which flowers grow
the slowest?
7 What colour are the
quietest birds?
8 What colour are the
noisiest birds?

4 **Listen and point to the picture.** 🎧

5 **Act out the story.**

6 **Write the words.**

_____ _____

_____ _____

_____ _____

165

Reading comprehension questions

Unit 1: pages 10–17: *Professor Inkspot's telescope*

Did Billy wake up early or late? What woke him up? Who lived next door? Where was Professor Inkspot's machine? What did the machine look like? (What did it have?) What did they see on the screen? Was the machine an interactive telescope? What was it? Who were the people on the screen?

Unit 2: pages 18–25: *Chinese Dragons*

Do Chinese people like dragons? In Chinese stories where did dragons come from? What did they bring? What colour were dragons? Were they big or small? In one old story a dragon helped a king. How many heads did the dragon have? Where did they meet every night? What did the king and the dragon talk about? Where did Chinese people put pictures of dragons?

Unit 3: pages 26–33: *The Aztecs of Central America*

Where did the Aztecs live? What did they build in lakes? What did they look for under the ground? Did children help in the house? What did children learn at school? What did the Aztecs build? What did important people like to wear? What was Aztec writing like? Who captured the Aztec city and the king?

Unit 4: pages 36–43: *Animals of the Gobi Desert*

What animals can you see in the Gobi desert? Which animals are wild? Which animals belong to the herdsmen? Where do the herdsmen go in the spring? What do they take with them? How many humps does a Bactrian camel have? Why do they have humps? Are gazelles fast or slow? Do snow leopards live alone or in groups? Are they dangerous to people? Which desert animals do you like?

Unit 5: pages 44–51: *The horse race*

Where did Sukhe and his family live? How many people were there in Sukhe's family? Was Sukhe older or younger than Shirav? Where did the family go one day? Why did they go there? How did they travel there? What was

the first race? Who rode in the race? Was Shirav a good rider? Was Sukhe's horse fast? Who won the race? Who came second? How did the boys' father feel after the race?

Unit 6: pages 52–59: *Ice age giants*

Where did people live in the Ice Age? How many Ice Age animals can you name? Which was the biggest animal on land? Why did it have a thick coat? How big was the giant sloth? Did other animals attack it? Why not? What was a glyptodon's tail like? How did it use its tail? Was the sabre-tooth cat smaller than a tiger? What do you know about its teeth? What do you think about the giant Ice Age animals?

Unit 7: pages 62–69: *Flight*

In the first poem is the sun shining? Are the birds flying away to a warm place or to a cool place? What are the birds going to see? Does the boy want to be like the birds? What does he want to do? In the second poem which animals were in the basket? What was under the balloon? What did the balloon do? What did it look like? What did everyone do when the balloon came down? Was it exciting?

Unit 8: pages 70–77: *Holiday island*

Where are the children spending their holiday? Do they go into a cave? What mustn't they do in the cave? Why not? Is it cold and dark or bright and warm in the cave? What can they smell? How many shells do they find? What do they hear in the cave? Is there a crab in the pool? Is the water cold or warm? What do they find in the pool? Can they keep it? What must they do?

Unit 9: pages 78–85: *A letter from a sailor*

What is Tom's job? Who is Harry? Where is the ship sailing to? What is the weather like? When did the storm happen? What was the wind like? What was the sea like? Did it rain? How long did the storm last? Did Tom sleep? Where did they go after the storm?
What did Tom see in the market? When are they going to arrive in India? What does Tom want to do there?

Unit 10: pages 88–95: *Pictures*

Where did people first paint pictures? Where could you see the story of a pharaoh's life? Did rich people or poor people have paintings in their homes? What was in these paintings? When did people start to take photographs? Which came first: colour photos or black and white photos? What can you do with a digital camera?

Unit 11: pages 96–103: *The diving lesson*

Where did Andy spend his holidays? Did his cousins like diving? Did Andy like diving? Could Andy swim? Could he put his head under the water? Why not? What did Uncle Roy find in the hut? Who showed Andy how to use the mask? What did Andy see under the water? How long was he swimming? Was he scared or did he like it?

Unit 12: pages 104–111: *Coral reefs*

Are corals plants or animals? How do corals grow? Can you name any corals? Where can you find many soft corals? Why does a parrotfish have this name? Are there any dangerous creatures on a coral reef? Can you describe them? Why are some coral reefs in danger? What did the crown-of-thorns starfish do? Where did this happen?

Unit 13: pages 114–121: *Millie's London diary*

What did Millie write about in her diary? Where does Mr Jolly work? What did Grandmother buy in his shop? Where does Aunt Sara live? What did Millie do at her house? What did Mr Brown bring for Millie and John? Where did they see the flower girl? What was she selling? Why does she often look unhappy? Where do they see the policeman? Can you describe his clothes?

Unit 14: pages 122–129: *The Romans*

Was the Roman Empire big or small? What did the Romans build? Why did the Romans build straight roads? What did a Roman soldier wear on his head? What did he wear on his feet? What did he carry? How many horses pulled a Roman chariot? Were Roman chariots light or heavy? What did Roman people like to watch? Why were chariot races dangerous?

Unit 15: pages 130–137: *Delicious ice cream*

In the first poem what does the poet dream of? What fruit does he like with ice cream? Where does he like to sit when he's eating ice cream? What can he do while he's eating ice cream? In the second poem what is on the lolly wrapper? Who bought it for the boy? What flavour is it? Does the boy eat it quickly or slowly? In the third poem how many ice cream flavours can you remember?

Unit 16: pages 140–147: *Glass*

What is glass made from? What happens when sand gets very hot? What were the first glass objects? What did the Egyptians make from glass? What glass objects did the Romans have in their homes? What does a glass blower do with his pipe? What happens to the glass? What does a glass blower do with a piece of wood?

Unit 17: pages 148–155: *Eddie, the Emerald Island Detective*

What did thieves steal from the museum? Why was Professor Trench in shock? Where did the police look for the vase? Who saw the thieves? What were they doing? How did the thieves hide the vase? Who did Eddie tell? Did the police catch the thieves? Did they find the vase? Whose picture was in the newspaper?

Unit 18: pages 156–163: *The selfish giant*

Where did the children play? Why was the giant away? When he saw the children in his garden, was he happy or angry? What did he build around his garden? Did spring come to the giant's garden? What was it like in his garden? What did the giant hear one morning? What did he see in the wall? What did he see in the trees? Was the giant happy or angry? What did he do to the wall?

Macmillan Education
Between Towns Road, Oxford OX4 3PP
A division of Macmillan Publishers Limited
Companies and representatives throughout the world

ISBN 978-1-4050-1369-7

Text © Mary Bowen, Louis Fidge, Liz Hocking and Wendy Wren 2006
Design and illustration © Macmillan Publishers Ltd 2006

First published 2006

Design and layout by Oliver Design and Wild Apple Design Ltd
Illustrated by Barking Dog Art, Juliet Breese, Kate Davies, Katy Jackson, Bill Toop,
David Till, Gary Wing
Cover design by Oliver Design

Printed and bound in Malaysia

2014 2013 2012 2011 2010
10 9 8

The authors and publishers are grateful for permission to reprint the following:

Veronica Clark 'Sea Dive' from *Birds and Beasts Animal songs, games and activities*
chosen by Sheena Roberts (A & C Black Ltd, 1987), copyright © A & C Black Limited
1987, reprinted by permission of the publisher.
John Emlyn Edwards 'The Lazy Coconut Tree' from *Ta Ra Ra Boom De Ay* by David
Gadsby and Beatrice Harrop (A & C Black Ltd, 1977), reprinted by permission of David
Higham Associates Limited.
Veronica Clark 'Blast Off' from *High low dolly pepper: Developing music skills with
young children* (A & C Black Ltd, 1991), copyright © Veronica Clark 1991, reprinted by
permission of the publisher.

Although we have tried to trace and contact copyright holders before publication, in
some cases this has not been possible. If contacted we will be pleased to rectify any
errors or omissions at the earliest opportunity

The authors and publishers would like to thank the following for permission to reproduce
their photographic material:

Alamy/Blickwinkle p36, Alamy/Motoring Picture Library p53 (tr&cr), Alamy/Transtock
Inc p59 (tr), Alamy/Dennis MacDonald p95 (tl), ALamy/Jeff Greenberg p95 (cr),
Alamy/Robert Stainforth p59 (bl), Alamy/Oote Boe p140, COrbis/Chris Hellier p18 (l),
Corbis/Asian Art & Technology, Inc p18 (r), Corbis/Christie's Images p19, Corbis/Jim
Zuckerman p60 (t), Corbis/John Henley p89 (cr), Corbis/Jolanda Cats & Hans
Withoos/Zefa p 102, FLPA/Michael & Patricia Fogden/Minden Pictures p52
(br),FLPA/Norbert Wu p53 (r), FLPA/Winifred Wisniewski p57 (tr), FLPA/D Parer & E
Parer-Cook/AUSCA/Minden Pictures p57 (cr), FLPA/Jurgen & Christine Sohns p57 (br),
FLPA/Ariadne Van Zandbergen p59 (br), FLPA/Jurgen & Christine Sohns p61 (t&b),
FLPA/Frans Lanting/Minden Pictures p68, FLPA/Panda Photo p111(tl), FLPA/R
Dirscherl p111 (bl&tr), FLPA/Chris Newbert/Minden Pictures p111 (br), FLPA/Mark
Newman p137 (tl), FLPA/R Dirscherl p137 (tr), FLPA/Jim Brandenburg/Minden Pictures
p137 (b), FLPA/Terry Andrewartha p137 (cr),Getty Images/Stuart Westmorland p104,
Getty Images/West Rock p109, Getty Images/Georgette Douwma p110, Nature Picture
Library/Doc White p57 (tl), Oxford Scientific Films/Karen Gowlett-Holmes p57 (cl),
Photolibrary/Adam Jones p42, Photolibrary/David Messent p84, Royalty Free/Getty
Images p52(cl), Royalty Free/Digital Vision p53(br), Royalty Free/Eye Wire p57(bl),
Science & Society Picture Library/NMPFT p89 (tr), Science & Society Picture
Library/Science Museum p89 (tc&br&bl)), Science & Society Picture Library/Science
Museum p90 (l&t&r), Science & Society Picture Library/NMPFT p90 (b).